LIBRARY SIGNAGE
AND WAYFINDING DESIGN

ALA Editions purchases fund advocacy, awareness, and accreditation programs for library professionals worldwide.

LIBRARY SIGNAGE
AND WAYFINDING DESIGN

*Communicating Effectively
with Your Users*

MARK AARON POLGER

WITHDRAWN

CHICAGO 2022

MARK AARON POLGER is associate professor and coordinator of library outreach at the College of Staten Island, City University of New York (CUNY). His responsibilities include coordinating the library's marketing and outreach activities, engaging in campus partnerships, promoting library events, and coordinating assessment of library services and resources. His research interests include library marketing, library signage, and user experience (UX) design. He is most interested in how users interact with the library's physical and virtual touch points; specifically, the website, signage, and promotional materials. He has written and presented on topics ranging from library marketing strategies, faculty outreach, library jargon, and library signage. Originally from Montreal, Canada, he moved to New York City in 2008.

© 2022 by the American Library Association

Extensive effort has gone into ensuring the reliability of the information in this book; however, the publisher makes no warranty, express or implied, with respect to the material contained herein.

ISBN: 978-0-8389-3785-3 (paper)

Library of Congress Cataloging-in-Publication Data

Names: Polger, Mark Aaron, author.
Title: Library signage and wayfinding design : communicating effectively with your users / Mark Aaron Polger.
Description: Chicago : ALA Editions, 2022. | Includes bibliographical references and index. | Summary: "This book provides tips and best practices for developing better library signage and provides guidance for creating a signage strategy"—Provided by publisher.
Identifiers: LCCN 2021027761 | ISBN 9780838937853 (paperback)
Subjects: LCSH: Library signs.
Classification: LCC Z679.57 P65 2022 | DDC 025.5/6—dc23
LC record available at https://lccn.loc.gov/2021027761

Book design by Kim Hudgins in the Bicyclette, Utopia, and Open Sans typefaces.
Cover image © sollia/Adobe Stock.

♾ This paper meets the requirements of ANSI/NISO Z39.48-1992 (Permanence of Paper).

Printed in the United States of America
26 25 24 23 22   5 4 3 2 1

This book is dedicated to my dear friend Keith M. Saks. We met only ten years ago, but you've been such an important person in my life. Thanks for being so wonderfully supportive on so many levels. Thanks for your humor, wit, sarcasm, and common sense. Thanks for supporting all my endeavors in life, including those frequent *New York Times* clippings on librarianship, vegan food, and Canadiana.

You be the best.

CONTENTS

Preface: My Fascination with Street Signs / ix
Acknowledgments / xiii
Introduction: Why Is Signage Important? / xv

A Brief History of Signs and Wayfinding | 1

Signage Research Methods | 15

Conducting a Signage Audit | 29

Digital Signage | 65

Signage Best Practices and Policies | 85

Signage and the Americans with Disabilities Act | 107

Conclusion: Practice What You Preach / 119
Index / 123

PREFACE

My Fascination with Street Signs

SINCE I WAS A CHILD, I WAS ALWAYS OBSESSED WITH STREET SIGNS AND maps. In each city I visited, the first item I picked up was a map so I could get acquainted with my whereabouts. I have always been spatially aware of my surroundings, and I have remained curious by exploring new cities by foot.

I grew up in Côte Saint-Luc, one of the many cities on the island of Montreal, in Quebec, the only French province in Canada. The island of Montreal has sixteen separate cities and towns. One of these is the city of Montreal, which itself has nineteen neighborhoods. Each of these municipalities have their own unique identity and local culture. The entire island of Montreal has its own public transit system that serves all the cities on the island.

Are you confused yet? I was. As a child who grew up speaking English, I had to learn how to navigate the city and the province, which is 80 percent French speaking. I was a curious kid who loved to explore the city on public transit. I started taking the local city bus at ten years old (it was the 1980s). I remember taking the bus to my elementary school, one city away, and feeling I was on an adventure. I was proud of myself for traveling to school alone. On my twenty-minute bus ride, I distinctly remember how the street signs changed in color, shape, and design. Along the bus route, the different street names informed me that I was moving from one city to another. Street signs not only identified the streets but symbolized each city's identity and place on the map. They also conveyed a deeper meaning, sometimes presenting political or social values. One such example was the renaming of Dorchester Street in Montreal. Rene Levesque, the premier of Quebec and founder of Le Parti Quebecois political party, died on November 1, 1987. The city of Montreal (not the island) decided to rename Dorchester Street to Boulevard Rene Levesque in his honor that same year (Fraser 1988). However, that street also passes through the city of Westmount, a mostly English-speaking community. To this day, the small portion of the street that runs through Westmount retains the name Dorchester Street. There are many more instances in Montreal where English street names have been renamed for important French-Canadian leaders.

In 1977, the province of Quebec enacted the Charter of the French Language, also known as Bill 101. This language law states that French is the official language of the province and that all written communications must be displayed in French first, with the French text double the size of the English text. This law applies to all aspects of social life, including the menus in restaurants, medical forms, signage, and advertisements (Kelly 2014). Transnational companies such as Kentucky Fried Chicken must follow the law; in the US, it is commonly branded as KFC, but in Quebec it is identified as "Poulet Frit Kentucky," shortened to PFK (Gade 2003). My parents both grew up in Montreal (pre–Bill 101), and they lived on streets with English street signs. Now those street names and signs are in French, although older generations still refer to them by their original English street names.

My fascination with street signs continued when I moved to Toronto in 2001. Toronto is the largest city in Canada, and before 1998, it was composed of six smaller cities: Etobicoke, Scarborough, York, East York, North York, and *old* Toronto. The cities merged in 1998 to form the "Toronto" *megacity,* but many years went by before the street signs began to show any visual consistency between the previously separate cities. During those years, I could easily identify the original city name based on their architecture and their street signs. Authors have cited 140 distinct neighborhoods in Toronto that prominently display branded street signage, funded by each Business Improvement Association (BIA; Bradburn 2014; City of Toronto 2020). Even the Toronto Public Library system reveals the city's histories. While the cities also merged their library systems, some branches still had signage referring back to their original home city. I worked at the Rexdale branch of the Toronto Public Library in 2002, but the signage still identified it as Etobicoke Public Libraries.

Since 2008, I have been living in New York City, and I have grown to appreciate its consistent street sign design. I live in the borough of Manhattan, where streets are organized into a grid. East-numbered streets are east of Fifth Avenue and west-numbered streets are west of Fifth Avenue. Fifth Avenue is the dividing line for most of the island. Street signs divide the city, providing directions and the approximate location of each residential or commercial building. For example, an address of 250 East 14th Street is approximately two and a half blocks east of Fifth Avenue, for each block represents 100 "address" numbers. Street signs and addresses also provide meaning to tourists and residents and mark the invisible borders between neighborhoods.[1]

Signs can provide deep levels of meaning and be playful at the same time: In 2016, when singer Prince passed away, New Yorkers redecorated Prince Street subway station in honor of his memory (Meier 2016). Recently, the station identification signage for the New York City subway was altered to commemorate singer Aretha Franklin and US Supreme Court Justice Ruth Bader Ginsburg after their deaths. Franklin Street subway stations (in the boroughs of Manhattan and Brooklyn) had *respect* decals added to their station identification signage to pay tribute to Franklin's life (Marcus, 2018), and the 50th Street station was recently renamed "Ruth Street" in honor of Ruth Bader Ginsburg.[2]

Signs are tools for meaning-making that direct people in how to understand phenomena. To serve this purpose, they should be clear, concise, easily understood, and intuitive. From a user experience (UX) perspective, they should be usable, useful, attractive, and purposeful. From an accessibility perspective, they should be compliant with the Americans with Disabilities Act (ADA), legible, and placed strategically. As one author says, it is better to have no signs than bad signs (White 2010). Signs aid the wayfinding experience, identify spaces, promote services and resources, inform policy, and may lessen anxiety and confusion.

In libraries, signs can decrease directional reference questions. However, too many signs can contribute to *visual noise*—sensory overload that can cause confusion, anxiety, worry, or apathy (Torbati 2016). Finally, bad signage does not serve its purpose, for it is often ignored, meaning that it does not convey its intended message to users. This book offers best practices, guidelines, ideas, and the necessary planning tools so that you can design and create more effective signage.

REFERENCES

Bradburn, Jamie. 2014. "A Short History of Toronto's Street Signs." May 28, 2014. https://torontoist.com/2014/05/a-short-history-of-torontos-street-signs/.

Cook, Lauren. 2020. "50th Street subway station renamed 'Ruth St.' to honor RBG." September 20, www.pix11.com/news/local-news/manhattan/50th-street-subway-station-renamed-ruth-st-to-honor-rbg/.

City of Toronto. 2020. "Neighbourhood Profiles and City of Toronto." September 19, 2020. www.toronto.ca/city-government/data-research-maps/neighbourhoods-communities/neighbourhood-profiles/.

Fraser, Matthew. 1988. "Publisher and, now at 64, mayor of Westmount May Cutler is one for the book." January 14, 1988. *Montreal Gazette.* https://advance-lexis-com.proxy.library.csi.cuny.edu/api/document?collection=news&id=urn:contentItem:4MH4-5J60-TXJ2-N0TW-00000-00&context=1516831.

Gade, Daniel W. 2003. "Language, Identity, and the Scriptorial Landscape in Quebec and Catalonia." *Geographical Review* 93, no. 4: 429–48.

Joseph, Richard. 2017. "The Myth of 'East of Adelaide.'" September 19, 2017. https://westerngazette.ca/opinion/the-myth-of-east-of-adelaide/article_49512eae-9d70-11e7-a1a0-cfdd82081747.html.

Kelly, Amanda. 2014. "Fact File: What Is Bill 101?" March 28, 2014. https://globalnews.ca/news/1237519/fact-file-what-is-bill-101/.

Marcus, Lilit. 2018. "Aretha Franklin Gets Respect from the NYC subway." September 3, 2018. www.cnn.com/travel/article/aretha-franklin-nyc-subway-tribute/index.html.

Meier, Allison. 2016. "The Most Beautiful Subway Station in the World: NYC Pays Tribute to Prince." April 22, 2016. https://hyperallergic.com/293082/the-most-beautiful-subway-station-in-the-world-nyc-pays-tribute-to-prince/.

Smith, Virginia K. 2016. "Shape-shifting NYC neighborhoods: Why Search Sites Differ on the Boundaries, and How It Affects Your Bottom line." September 12, 2016. www.brickunderground.com/neighborhoodintel/how-NYC-neighborhood-boundaries-get-muddled/.

Torbati, Ali. 2016. "Reducing Visual Noise for a Better User Experience." October 21, 2016. https://uxdesign.cc/reducing-visual-noise-for-a-better-user-experience-ae3407ff9c99.

White, Leah L. 2010. "Signage: Better None Than Bad." *American Libraries* 41, no. 8: 23.

NOTES

1. It should be noted that neighborhood borders are always changing in New York City, and street names and signs are usually the first identifiers of these neighborhood borders. Neighborhood names have changed over the years and some of them are even invented by realtors (Smith 2016).
2. It is likely that this is not a permanent name change but a temporary signal of respect, conveyed by public signage (Cook 2020).

ACKNOWLEDGMENTS

THANKS TO MY EDITOR HEATH SLEDGE FOR BEING WONDERFULLY PATIENT and supportive throughout the process of this book project. Thanks to Jamie Santoro at ALA Editions for believing in this project from the very beginning. Thanks to Dan Freeman and Colton Ursiny for inviting me back each year to present my annual webinars on library signage for ALA eLearning Solutions. Thanks to my parents Leona and David Polger, who have been so supportive throughout my career and life.

Thanks to Janice Rosen, Archives Director of the Alex Dworkin Canadian Jewish Archives in Montreal, Canada. I worked for Janice from 1993–99 before attending library school, and she was my favorite boss. She has continued to be a wonderful mentor and friend twenty-eight years later.

Thanks to Kathy Dempsey, founding chair of the Library Marketing and Communications Conference, editor of *Marketing Library Services*, my library marketing mentor, and my friend. We both share a passion for thinking about the library user first, before jumping into a marketing opportunity. I was so happy to present my signage research at the 2016 Library Marketing and Communications Conference.

Thanks to my small network of friends and family in Montreal, Toronto, and New York City; Keith Saks, Vivian Bejerman, Kinga Breining, Peter Kiss, Wendy Furtenbacher, Don Madonna, Karen Okamoto, Antonio D'Souza, Elizabeth (Lisa) Palov, Mason Cooper, Maxine D'Alfonso, Beth Hurley, David Abecassis, Aaron Boros, Daniel Malen, Marlin Roy, Dimitry Epelbaum, Susan Yegendorf, Susanne Marcus Solomkin, Lynn Marcus, Shari Kopla, Jana Stuart, Christy Sich, Dan Sich, Joel Moses, Heidi Furtenbacher, and Naomi Gold.

Thanks to Amy F. Stempler, Associate Dean and Chief Librarian at the College of Staten Island (CSI) Library for supporting my signage research endeavors. We started conducting studies on our library's signage many years ago and have collaborated and presented our research at many professional conferences and have written articles in academic journals. I believe that we both have made our library more attractive, welcoming, and uncluttered with more user-friendly signage. I would like to thank the CSI Library Personnel and Budgetary (P&B) Committee who granted me research leave in the summers of 2019 and 2020 so I could complete this book project. Lastly, I'd like to thank the many libraries who contributed their library's signage policies and their *before and after* images of their library signage audits.

INTRODUCTION

Why Is Signage Important?

WE LIVE IN A SOCIETY THAT IS SATURATED WITH VISUALS: ADVERTISING, television, film, visual arts, the World Wide Web, and social media. Signs are part of this visual landscape. They are a series of stimuli, and the reaction they provoke should fulfill the sign's purpose. They provide assistance in wayfinding and help people navigate through physical spaces. They should give users a sense of confidence; signs may serve as inferential cues, and poorly designed signs may reflect poorly on the organization. Signage is thus one of the most important components of marketing communications. Signs need not be text-heavy to be effective, for as a visual medium they can convey a compelling message with a few words and an attractive image.

All signs should attract attention, be welcoming, useful, friendly, and most importantly, informative. Signs communicate messages and enable users to navigate, learn, and make decisions. An environment without signs may cause confusion, anxiety, and worry. Signs bring life to any airport, highway, shopping mall, sports complex, college campus, bus terminal, train station, office building, and library. They provide identification, evoke policies and procedures, promote, advertise, and provide directions.

Signs are particularly important in the library, for the library building is a space where users go to learn. They may visit the facility to borrow materials, study, read, or conduct research. Upon entering the building, users must make decisions about where and how to accomplish the purpose for their visit. Signage can help reduce library anxiety and create a more positive user experience. However, too many signs can produce information overload, causing anxiety and confusion.

Kellaris and Machleit (2016) propose a conceptual framework for signage, with five elements:

- signage design
- user personality traits
- contextual variables such as placement
- mediating processes
- response variables (cognitive, affective, and behavioral)

Signage design should follow current best practices in information design. *User personality traits* that may affect signage include the user's age, their familiarity with the space, their internal state, their motivational state, and their level of attention. *Contextual variables* include how the sign is placed: the distance, angle or perspective and its relationship to its surroundings. *Mediating processes* are the intended users' ability to process and/or understand the sign, which may affect the sign's color, font, and other design features. The *response variables* include users' thoughts, emotions, and concrete actions.

Signage falls into the broader practice of information design—the study of how to present information effectively. The concept of information design originated shortly after the print revolution: during the American revolution. William Playfair invented different types of graphs and charts on political and economic topics; Florence Nightingale invented different statistical graphs for public policy purposes; and Michael George Muhall and Otto Neurath developed pictorial statistics (Horn 1999).

While information design is largely considered to be the province of graphic designers, it's also important to multiple other professions, such as web designers, librarians, architects, museum curators, urban planners, UX designers, user interface designers, writers of instruction manuals, and computer programmers. Many materials require good information design, such as maps, infographics, diagrams, charts, data tables, indexes, and controlled vocabulary lists.

In libraries, signage with good information design is particularly crucial because services and resources must be identified and promoted to different user groups. Library signs have many functions, but for the purposes of this book, they will be divided into three broad categories: promotional, policy, and wayfinding signage. Signage serves many other functions, such as informational, instructional, and identification.

Terms Used in This Book (in Alphabetical Order)

A/B Testing
A/B testing is usually associated with UX for websites. This involves showing participants two slight variations (of a design) and asking them questions about its content and design and comparing the results. This can directly be applied to both print and digital signage (Schmidt and Etches 2014).

Aspect Ratio
The aspect ratio describes the relationship of an image's width and height. For example, a 16:9 aspect ratio is an image that is sized at 16 units width and 9 units in height. This typically corresponds to a resolution of 1,920 by 1,080 for a high definition (HD) widescreen monitor (Clem 2018).

Branding
Branding is the organization's visual identity. It represents the spirit of the organization. It extends beyond the logo and symbols and is closely tied to the organization's story or narrative. It is the sum of all the feelings associated with the organization. Branding is not tangible, as it relates to the uniqueness, values, and strengths of the organization. Other terms related to branding include brand loyalty, brand strength, and brand awareness. In this book, branding needs to be considered when designing and updating new library signage.

Built Environment
The built environment is any manufactured structure that is to be used for any human activity. Built environments are usually in urban centers and include train stations, airports, office buildings, municipal buildings, college campuses, shopping malls, hospitals, parks, subway stations, bus terminals, museums, community centers, and libraries (Harris 2010).

Color Contrast
Color contrast is the difference in brightness between the colors in the foreground and background. For signage to be ADA compliant, there needs to be at least 70 percent contrast (United States Department of Justice 2010). Contrast can also be applied to typeface or font size.

Communications
Communications relates to how organizations share meaning with their users. It can be achieved through print, digital images, web content, radio, telephone,

television, and on social media. Signage is one of many communication channels where information gets disseminated. Kotler (1982, 355) describes the communication process as two-way, with a sender and receiver. Communication involves eight parts:

1. sender conveys a message
2. message is sent and encoded by the recipient
3. message itself is the verbal, written, or nonverbal symbols
4. message is sent through different communication channels (or path)
5. message is decoded through a process by which the receiver understands and processes the message
6. message is received
7. reactions of those who have received the message(s)
8. receiver's response to the message(s)

Content Management System (CMS)
A CMS is a robust software program used to coordinate the dissemination of flow of information using a backend database. Most large websites use a CMS to organize and manage their individual web pages. A CMS is used to separate content from design. Common CMSs include Drupal, Joomla, and WordPress. Although CMSs are usually associated with website management, they can be used to manage digital signage. Drupal, for example, is used to manage both the website and network of digital signage for the MTA New York City Transit System (Madison 2019).

Copy
The term *copy* refers to the text that is used for marketing and advertising purposes. Copy is the written material that is used to spread a specific marketing message. In the context of this book, copy is the signage message, which is the text used that accompanies the image.

Decision Points (or Nodes, Touch Points, or Bump Points)
Throughout the literature of signage, wayfinding, and UX design, the terms *touch points, bump points, nodes,* or *decision points* are used synonymously. For the purposes of this book, decision points will be used. In wayfinding research, it relates to a point where a user must make a decision. This is usually found at intersections in the built environment. In UX research, the term *touch point* is used to describe any element of the system which the user comes into contact. It represents the pathway that the user makes during their journey in your organization. They are important for both UX and wayfinding research because they

relate to how users navigate through virtual and physical spaces and the decisions they make (Brugnoli 2009).

Digital Signage
Digital signage uses different technology, such as LCD, LED, plasma, projection, and e-paper, to display digital images, video, audio, text, and web content on a screen. It is often associated with out-of-home (OOH) advertising. Digital signage can either be static or dynamic. Static digital signage refers to static images or text. Dynamic digital signage examples include scrolling images, social media feeds, video, animation, or interactive content (Lafitte 2019).

Dots Per Inch (DPI)
DPI refers to the number of printed dots contained within one inch of an image printed by a printer. It differs from pixels per inch (PPI). DPI is used to determine the print size of an image on paper. PPI is used to determine the quality of a digital image on screen (Sony Support 2019).

Dwell Time
This is the amount of time that users pay attention to signage. Measurement tools such as eye trackers estimate that the average person glances at a sign for 0.7–0.9 seconds (Condomaros 2019).

Endcap (or Endcap Displays)
In merchandising, endcap displays are the print and digital signage screens at the end of the aisle or hallway or corridor. They are used to promote and highlight specific products in a retail setting and to grab a customer's attention (Gilbert 2019).

Focus Groups
Focus groups are a qualitative research method that comprise a small group of participants who provide an open-ended dialogue on the subject matter. This type of research technique provides the most rich and robust data but is the most time consuming and costly (Schmidt and Etches 2014).

High Definition (HD)
Harding (2020) describes HD as any screen with a resolution of 720p (1,280 by 720 pixels) or more. Standard definition (SD) has a resolution of 640 by 480 pixels; 1,920 by 1,080 pixels are known as full high definition (FHD); 2,560 by 1,440 is 2K; and 3,840 by 2,160 pixels is 4K (or Ultra HD).

Kerning

Kerning is the space between the letters. Spacing your letters too closely will make the copy very hard to read. If the spaces between the letters are too far apart, they will look like two separate words. Most design programs have automated kerning, but a signage designer may opt to manually kern the letters. If a particular word does not look right, it is recommended to turn the word upside down to examine the spacing between the letters. Always kern in chunks of three, which is easier than tackling an entire line of text (Dennis 2017).

Leading

Leading is the vertical spacing between lines of text. Also known as line spacing, the recommend leading at 20 percent of the font size is the recommended practice (Dennis 2017).

Marketing Message

The marketing *message* is the intended communications to that target audience. For the purposes of this book, the message is the unified communication that is informed by a library's marketing plan and signage policy. Kotler (1982, 361) describes the message by managing to get attention, hold interest, arouse desire, and obtain action, known as the AIDA model.

Market Research

Market research describes the different types of research techniques that can be utilized to study your target audience. For the purposes of clarity, it is synonymous with user research. In this book, many different user research techniques will be discussed and shown how they can be applied to signage and wayfinding. Some are specific to the discipline of UX design and some are broader in nature.

Persona

Personas come from UX research and they represent a profile of a fictional individual who is a member of a specific user community. A persona is an archetype of a target user of a product or service. Personas are similar to segments (see definition of *segmentation* below), but they differ slightly. They are fictionalized profiles of individuals with specific characteristics, whereas segments are user groups who share common characteristics, values, and beliefs. Some conflate the terms *personas* and *segments*, but Harley (2015) argues that personas are more personal, individualized, and specific than segments.

Pixels

Pike (2017) explains that *pixel* comes from "picture element." She states that they are the dots that build an image. The more pixels there are in a given space and the closer they are, the clearer the image. If the pixels are large and spaced apart, then the image is said to be pixelated, which means the pixels are visible to the naked eye. Pixelated images tend to look blurry.

Pixels Per Inch (PPI)
PPI refers to the number of pixels contained within one inch of an image displayed on a computer monitor (Pike 2017; Sony Support 2019).

Resolution
Rusen (2019) states that resolution is the number of pixels per unit of area, rather than the total number of pixels. It usually describes the number of pixels arranged horizontally and vertically on a monitor. The common name (4K, 5K, etc.) is associated with the horizontal display resolution size. Table 0.1 provides a list of the resolution names and screen sizes.

TABLE 0.1
Common resolution names and their resolutions

Common Name	Resolution
5K	5,120 × 2,880
Ultrahigh definition (UHD) or 4K	3,840 × 2,160
Quad high definition (QHD)	2,560 × 1,440
2K	2,048 × 1,080
Widescreen ultraextended graphics array (WUXGA)	1,920 × 1,200
Full high definition (Full HD)	1,920 × 1,080
High definition (HD)	1,280 × 720

Segmentation
Segmentation describes how marketers group their audience into smaller groups based on similarities, whether those similarities are demographic or based on needs, desires, or expectations. A similar term that describes the grouping of different users is *personas*. Segmentation is directly related to how library employees develop marketing activities that are aimed to a specific target audience (Yeo 2005).

Sign versus Signage
Brown (1995) writes that signage is the system (or network) of many signs which

work together in tandem. A signage system is one that is consistent in colors, shapes, sizes, and messages. Where a sign stands alone with a single message, signage is a system that is affected by lighting, the building interiors, stairways, hallways, entrances, and exits.

Signage Audit
A signage audit is an evaluative method used to take an inventory of your signage for analysis, reflection, and improvement. An audit may involve taking an inventory of the current signs, classifying the signs into categories, evaluating its current message, visual appeal, physical condition, and placement. An audit may involve the complete removal and replacement of all signs.

Signage Policy
A signage policy is an official document with a system of principles and rules that inform the design, content, placement, and maintenance of signage. A signage policy is more formalized, while guidelines are recommendations.

Tactile Signage
Tactile signage is any sign system that can be read by touch. Examples of tactile signage may include Braille, raised print, and raised symbols. Doors and openings that lead to public spaces should be identified by tactile signage (United States Department of Justice 2010).

Tracking
While kerning is the spacing between the individual letterforms, tracking uniformly adjusts the spacing over a range of characters. Both kerning and tracking are in graphic design to provide a more aesthetically pleasing arrangement in the layout of the copy (Mapp 2014).

Typeface
Typeface is the overall design of a collection of fonts. It is the overall aesthetic and includes the unified look for all of the lettering, numbers, and symbols of that font family. Typeface is to parent as font is to child. A typeface informs the overall style of the font. Each typeface has a family of fonts that differ in qualities (some fonts are bold, italics, or condensed). For Roman typefaces, the two main types are serif and sans serif typefaces. Serif types have edges at the end of most of its letters. Sans serif typefaces have no edge strokes at the tips of the font. Serif types are typically used for large bodies of text (i.e., books) and sans serif types is used for large-scale signs, posters, brochures, and web-based materials (Keung 2020).

Typography
Typography is the design, arrangement, and display of different typefaces to make written language readable and attractive. Typography encompasses the concepts of typefaces, type classification, and type styles. They relate to more specific elements such as fonts, characters, numbers, color, size, punctuation, borders, and figures. Typography differs from calligraphy because one focuses on mass production (of texts) and the other relates to single, handwritten copies (Craig 2008; Redish 2012).

User Experience (UX) Design
UX design is a collection of principles and practices used when designing physical and virtual spaces. It represents the emotional feelings and perceptions when a user interacts and engages in a physical or virtual interface. Although UX design is often associated with websites, it can be applied to physical spaces. It involves different types of user research that investigate all facets of the physical and virtual spaces. UX design merges usability with user-centered empathy to create physical and virtual spaces that are usable, useful, and desirable (Schmidt and Etches 2014).

Viewing Distance
Viewing distance is the optimal distance between the user and the display. There is much disagreement in a standardized formula determining the optimal viewing distance between a user and a sign. Factors such as the text height (point font), the size of the display screen, and the display resolution influence the ideal viewing distance.

Wayfinding
Wayfinding refers to how people navigate their way around physical space. Wayfinding is cross disciplinary as it relates to graphic design, architecture, cognitive psychology, and environmental studies. It is experiential in nature and it comprises the sociocultural and emotional experience of navigating a physical space in urban centers (Symonds, Brown, and Lo Iacono 2017). It is the ability to know where you are, where you are headed, the best route to take, know when you have arrived, and know how to exit (Apelt, Crawford, and Hogan 2007).

How to Navigate This Book

Chapter 1 provides a brief history of signage and wayfinding by connecting signs to advertising and modern publishing, as well as typography and graphic design. This chapter also provides a brief overview of Saussure's and Peirce's semiotic theories of signs, defining the term *sign* and differentiating it from signals and symbols.

Chapter 2 illustrates signage research techniques and methods used to gather library users' perceptions, feelings, and attitudes toward signage.

Chapter 3 lays out how to undertake a signage audit and provides examples of signage "before" and "after" examples of an audit.

Chapter 4 provides an overview of digital signage, digital signage hardware (displays, media players), content management software that controls signage content, and the different design software used to create digital signs. It also includes a brief discussion of digital signage companies, a select list of signage hardware and software companies, and examples of digital signage partnerships between publicly funded organizations and private corporations.

Chapter 5 provides best practice signage guidelines and examples of library signage policies.

Chapter 6 describes guidelines in developing library signage that is ADA compliant.

REFERENCES

Apelt, Ron, John Crawford, and David J. Hogan. 2007. *Wayfinding Design Guidelines*. Brisbane: CRC for Construction Innovation.

Brown, Carol R. 1995. *Planning Library Interiors: The Selection of Furnishings for the 21st Century*. Phoenix: Oryx Press.

Brugnoli, Gianluca. 2009. "Connecting the Dots of User Experience." *Journal of Information Architecture* 1, no. 1: 6–15.

Calori, Chris, and David Vanden-Eynden. 2015. *Signage and Wayfinding Design: A Complete Guide to Creating Environmental Graphic Design Systems*. Hoboken, NJ: John Wiley & Sons.

Clem, Alex. 2018. "A Guide to Common Aspect Ratios, Image Sizes, and Photograph Sizes." Shutterstock blog, August 2, 2018. www.shutterstock.com/blog/common-aspect-ratios-photo-image-sizes/.

Condomaros, Christina. 2019. "Digital Signage Dwell Time: Secrets That Will Lead You to Success." Yodeck, May 16, 2019. www.yodeck.com/news/digital-signage-dwell-time/.

Cooper, Holly L. 2006. "A Brief History of Tactile Writing Systems for Readers with Blindness and Visual Impairments." *See/Hear* 11, no. 2. www.tsbvi.edu/seehear/spring06/history.htm.

Craig, Robert L. 2008. "Typography." In *The International Encyclopedia of Communication*, edited by Wolfgang Donsbach, 5193–97. Vol. 11. Malden, MA: Blackwell.

Datig, Ilka. 2015. "Walking in Your Users' Shoes: An Introduction to User Experience Research as a Tool for Developing User-Centered Libraries." *College and Undergraduate Libraries* 22, no. 3–4: 234–46.

Dennis, Amy. 2017. "Kerning, Leading, and Tracking." Nice Branding, June 1, 2017. https://nice-branding.com/graphic-design-firm-spacing/.

Gilbert, Darren. 2019. "End Cap Display 101: Here's Everything You Need to Know." Dot Activ blog, May 31, 2019. www.dotactiv.com/blog/end-cap-display.

Harding, Scharon. 2020. "What Is 720p? HD Resolution Explained." Tom's Hardware, January 20, 2020. www.tomshardware.com/reviews/what-is-hd,5745.html.

Harley, Aurora. 2015. "Personas Make Users Memorable for Product Team Members." Nielsen Norman Group, February 16, 2015. www.nngroup.com/articles/persona/.

Harris, Richard. 2010. "Built Environment." In *Encyclopedia of Geography*, edited by Barney Warf, 298–300. Vol. 1. SAGE Reference. Gale Virtual Reference Library. https://link-gale-com.proxy.library.csi.cuny.edu.

Horn, Robert E. 1999. "Information Design: Emergence of a New Profession." In *Information Design*, edited by Robert Jacobson, 15–33. Cambridge, MA: MIT Press.

Kellaris, James J., and Karen A. Machleit. 2016. "Signage as Marketing Communication: A Conceptual Model and Research Propositions." *Interdisciplinary Journal of Signage and Wayfinding* 1, no. 1: 1–17.

Keung, Laura. 2020. "A Brief History of Display Fonts." Envato Tuts, July 27, 2020. https://design.tutsplus.com/articles/a-brief-history-of-display-fonts--cms-33518/.

Kotler, Philip, and Sidney J. Levy. 1969. "Broadening the Concept of Marketing." *Journal of Marketing* 33, no. 1: 10–15.

Kotler, Philip. 1982. *Marketing for Nonprofit Organizations*. Englewood Cliffs, NJ: Prentice-Hall.

Lafitte, Bomme. 2019. "What Is Digital Signage? The Most Accurate Definition." Intuiface blog, April 3, 2019. www.intuiface.com/blog/what-is-digital-signage/.

Loda, Marsha D. 2014. "Suggesting a More Effective Way to Use the Promotional Mix in Services." *Services Marketing Quarterly* 35, no. 4: 304–20.

Madison, Mike. 2019. "Using Drupal 8 and AWS IoT to Power Digital Signage for New York's Subway System." Acquia blog, January 20, 2019. https://dev.acquia.com/blog/using-drupal-8-and-aws-iot-to-power-digital-signage-for-new-yorks-subway-system/01/10/2018/20051/.

Mapp, Mark. 2014. "Importance of Kerning and Tracking." DaBrian Marketing blog, February 14, 2014. https://dabrianmarketing.com/blog/web-design/importance-kerning-tracking-creative-design/.

Pike, Jennifer. 2017. "Pixels, Resolution, and Aspect Ratio: What Does It All Mean?" Metova, October 2, 2017. https://metova.com/pixels-resolution-aspect-ratio-what-does-it-all-mean/.

Rowley, Jennifer. 1998. "Promotion and Marketing Communications in the Information Marketplace." *Library Review* 47, no. 8: 383–87.

Rusen, Ciprian Adrian. 2019. "What Do the 720p, 1080p, 1440p, 2K, 4K Resolutions Mean? What Are the Aspect Ratio and Orientation?" Digital Citizen, July 3, 2019. www.digitalcitizen.life/what-screen-resolution-or-aspect-ratio-what-do-720p-1080i-1080p-mean/.

Sassoon, Rosemary, and Albertine Gaur. 1997. *Signs, Symbols and Icons: Pre-History to the Computer Age*. Exeter: Intellect Books.

Schmidt, Aaron, and Amanda Etches. 2014. *Useful, Usable, Desirable*. Chicago: ALA Editions.

Shabluk, Mike. 2019. "An Overview of California ADA Signage Requirements." Erie Custom Signs, May 30, 2019. https://eriecustomsigns.com/an-overview-of-california-ada-signage-requirements/.

Sony Support. 2019. "What Is the Difference between Dots Per Inch (DPI) and Pixels Per Inch (PPI)?" Sony, August 21, 2019. www.sony.com/electronics/support/articles/00027623/.

Symonds, Paul, David H. K. Brown, and Valeria Lo Iacono. 2017. "Wayfinding as an Embodied Sociocultural Experience." *Sociological Research Online* 22, no. 1: 1–20.

United States Department of Justice. 2010. *2010 ADA Standards for Accessible Design*. https://www.ada.gov/regs2010/2010ADAStandards/2010ADAStandards.pdf/.

Yeo, Geoffrey. 2005. "Understanding Users and Use: A Market Segmentation Approach." *Journal of the Society of Archivists* 26, no. 1: 25–53.

1
A Brief History of Signs and Wayfinding

ACCORDING TO *WEBSTER'S NEW WORLD DICTIONARY* (1970), THE etymology of the word *sign* comes from the Latin word *signum* and is related to the words *signal* and *signify*. Signs convey messages and are visual communication tools that are used to direct people's attention. Signs convey meaning through symbols, text, and images. Hoch (2013) writes that the word also has French origins with the word *enseigne*, which means *signal* or *signboard*. The word is also connected to signify, signature, signatory, and significance.

In American Sign Language (ASL), *signing* is a form of communication—individuals use different hand and facial gestures and movements to convey meaning. The term *sign* is both a noun and verb. It is a symbol that refers people to specific phenomena, but it also entails the act of creating meaning and symbols for others to decode and understand (Taub 2001).

A sign uses symbols, color, text, and graphics to attract attention and provide information, but it also needs to be correctly decoded and interpreted by its intended audience (Eco 1984). Signs are communication tools that produce meaning. They come from the larger discipline of semiotics. Semiotics is the study of symbols and meaning in communication. Semiotics branches out into the following subdisciplines: analogy, allegory, metonymy, metaphor, symbolism, signification, and communication. *Biosemiotics* comes from the Greek term *sēmeiōtikos*, "observant of signs" (Jensen 2008).

A Theory of Signs

Charles Sanders Peirce

Peirce defined a sign as anything that can be interpreted by someone else (Zeman 1977). Signs do not carry meaning unless we make meaning out of them. Peirce argued that signs have a triadic relationship. This relationship is between the *representamen* (signifying element), the *object*, and the *interpretant*. The *representamen* is the medium used to transmit the message. The *interpretant* is the user (or the community of users) who decodes the meaning of the sign. The *object* represents the symbols used to convey the message in a sign.

Chandler (2019) provides the example of the red light as a sign for vehicles to stop at an intersection. The red light is the representamen, the vehicles stopping are the objects, and the meaning of the red light is the interpretant. His theory of signs was based on logic and informed a comprehensive system to communicating knowledge and meaning. He argued that people interpret signs based on those three components (Atkin 2010).

Because signs denote meaning, they are deconstructed by interpretants, and they (the interpretants) become a further sign. This semiotic process of meaning-making is infinite until a final sign is created that would terminate the semiotic process.

Peirce divided signs (as they relate to a *signifying element*), into three categories: qualities, existential facts, and laws (*qualisigns, sinsigns,* and *legisigns*). Every sign is either a quality, a fact, or a norm or law. Signs are further divided by how they are affected by the *object*. Signs are further divided into three categories: *icon, index,* and *symbol*. Icons resemble specific images, an index has a causal relationship, and symbols are related to their object (Atkin 2010).

Peirce further divided signs as they relate to the interpretant. They are divided into three categories: *rheme, dicent,* and *delome*. If a sign determines an interpretant by focusing our understanding based on qualitative features, then the sign is a *rheme*. If a sign determines an interpretant by focusing on existential features, then the sign is a *dicent*. If a sign determines an interpretant by focusing on conventional features, then the sign is a *delome* (Atkin 2010).

Peirce's theories later evolved, and his triad of *signifying element, object,* and *interpretant* were further divided into more categories. He further divided the *object* into *immediate object* and *dynamic object*. He further divided the *interpretant* into the following three: immediate interpretant, dynamic interpretant, and final interpretant.

Other variations of Peirce's triadic relationship are also known as the semiotic triangle; the *sign vehicle*, the *sense*, and the *referent*. In the above example of the red light, the red light is the sign vehicle, the sense is the stopped vehicle, and the referent is what the red light stands for—stop (Chandler 2019).

Ferdinand De Saussure

Saussure asserted that signs comprise a two-way psychological relationship of the signifier and the signified. Whether expressed as words or images, signs create meaning when placed within the context of a larger signage system. He believed that signs have no meaning without their signifier and signified. The signifier is the media format, which a person can sense, and the signified is the meaning that is interpreted. The signifier and signified unite to create the sign. The sign's purpose and objective are articulated within a social context (Chandler 2019). Furthermore, Chandler (2019) cites Louis Hjelmslev, who argues that a sign can be broken down into *form* and *content*. The content is the meaning of the sign (*signified*) and the form (*signifier*) is the container that is the vehicle that conveys this meaning. Saussure also introduces the concept of *signification*, which is the relationship between the sign and other signs within the system (Chandler 2019). Within a language, one signifier can refer to multiple signifieds and vice versa; one signified can originate from multiple signifiers (Chandler 2019, para. 20). The Saussurean model has been criticized by some scholars because it detaches the sign's meaning from its social context (Barnouw 1981). Although the relationship between the signifier and signified is often arbitrary, Chandler (2019) argues that it does depend on the social and cultural conventions.

Jean Baudrillard extended the idea that signs can also depict hyperreality and falsehoods, and he discussed how copies can look more realistic than the original (Giradin 1974). Roland Barthes (1970) argued that signs can have connotations and denotations, which means they can allude to a specific cultural context, and they can be literal or subtle in meaning. He argued that the modern world is built on meaning based on signs and symbols. Sign language, which falls outside the scope of this book, is a visual, spatial, and gestural language that uses hand, body, and face gestures to signify meaning. It's part of a larger communication system. Like physical signs in an airport, highway, shopping mall, or library, sign language creates meaning through hand, body, and face movements.

A Brief History of Signs

The history of signage can be traced back to 35,000 BCE, with the use of iconography, the ability to formulate and record thoughts using graphic symbols. Iconographic markings on wood, cloth, or stone were used to document information and support memory (Sassoon and Gaur 1997), and the earliest map (another graphic representation for sharing information) was a Babylonian clay tablet from 2300 BCE. Modern signs carrying text were made possible by the advent of movable type printing, invented in Europe by German blacksmith

Johannes Gutenberg in 1439. Similar innovations were also taking place outside of Europe. In the third century CE, the Chinese carved letters into wood blocks for printing (Berger 2014). In 1045 CE, Pi Sheng of China may have developed the first handset that made multiple copies of individual letters, which were cast so they could be printed with other letters—another form of movable type. In the early 1400s, King Sejong, a Korean scholar, developed a phonetic alphabet that propelled movable type and expanded book printing (and literacy) in Korea (Craig 2008).

The printing press revolutionized the dissemination of information in the fifteenth century. Printing was less time consuming and more cost effective than hand copying manuscripts. Texts became more common and more affordable, giving readers more access to books, increasing mass literacy. This would lead eventually to the Protestant reformation, the Enlightenment, and the scientific revolution.

The advent of print also jump-started the beginning of commercial publishing and the advertising industry (Samuelson 2000). Signage has been used for advertising in some form or another since ancient times. Both Ancient Greece and Rome had signboards of stone or terra-cotta that communicated information, and some Roman signs contained persuasive messages painted on walls in black or red (Presbrey 1929). As early as China's Song Dynasty (960 CE to 1127 CE), the country was found to have produced retail signage for their White Rabbit brand sewing needles (Petty, 2016). In Europe, modern advertising signage began with visual iconography in the fourteenth century, before the printing press; Richard III of England required shop owners to create signs identifying their businesses. Businesses created attractive symbols (i.e., logos) to distinguish their business from others (Landis 2017). During this period, signs were usually associated with inns and taverns, but in sixteenth-century London, manufacturers began to adapt their coats of arms into advertising signs.

In the mid-nineteenth century, in the midst of the Industrial Revolution, newly invented tools removed some of the technological limitations on mass-producing signage: the tracing pantograph and router created new fonts much more easily, and color lithographic printing allowed the production of large-scale billboards and signs. This was a particularly important and timely development because cities were rapidly expanding and mass transit was common; office buildings and train stations needed large-scale signage for wayfinding.

Classical serif fonts were still being designed until the twentieth century, but more modern, sans serif fonts began to appear in the 1920s, like the Futura font, designed by Paul Renner in 1927. This font was sleek and modern and was stripped of the classical features of a traditional serif font. These fonts were inspired by both the Bauhaus movement and the Art Deco movement of the

1920s. Commercial signs began to incorporate this font in restaurants, government buildings, hotels, airports, and stores (Berger 2014).

In the 1920s, the United States created a design manual known as the *Manual and Specifications for the Manufacture, Display, and Erection of U.S. Standard Road Markers and Signs*. It mandated specific typefaces such as Highway Gothic and Clearview for highway signs. Today, highways, airports, and train stations use a sans serif typeface similar to the Gothic type family. In the 1950's, the Univers and Helvetica fonts were established by Adrian Frutiger and Max Miedinger with Eduard Hoffmann respectively (Berger 2014).

Wayfinding

Wayfinding is the cognitive and spatial process of orienting oneself to a space and then navigating within it—figuring out where you are, where you want to go, and how you will get there (Dalton, Holscher, and Montello 2019). Since the explosive growth of cities and commercial architecture, wayfinding has been a key goal of signage. Many public spaces like airports, hospitals, train stations, bus terminals, shopping malls, and large department stores have sophisticated wayfinding systems in place—so sophisticated that people using these spaces do not even notice them. Good wayfinding systems enable people to seamlessly get from point A to point B. IKEA, the famous Swedish furniture store, is a perfect example. The store itself is a labyrinth, but it has a clear, accessible, well-designed navigation system, including you-are-here maps, clear signage, floor markings, and clear pathways that help customers navigate their way from the entrance through the store to the cashiers and exit (Mackereth 2020).

Modern wayfinding research goes back to the 1960s, when urban planners attempted to humanize modern urban spaces. In his book *The Image of the City*, Kevin Lynch (1960) coined the term to describe how people form a mental map of their own surroundings. Lynch found that most people's mental maps involve the following five components:

1. paths (streets, bus, and subway routes)
2. edges (physical barriers of walls, fences, and rivers)
3. districts (specific, memorable places)
4. nodes (known as touch points)
5. landmarks (physical structures that stand out in a built environment)

Paths provide the structure and framework for wayfinding. *Edges* mark the boundaries from one region to another, shaping the physical space and guiding people as they navigate paths. *Districts* represent distinct spaces that share common traits. (In a library, each library floor and each zone within the library might be seen as districts. Some floors comprise only book stacks, while others have large collaborative workspaces with expansive tables; various zones such as the silent study zone, the soft conversation zone, and the more social [loud] zone where collaboration and group work take place are also separate districts.) *Nodes* are the intersections where users make decisions: the book uses the terms nodes, bump points, touch points, and decision points synonymously. *Landmarks* are specific reference points that help the user navigate (Lynch 1960).

Wayfinding has been around long before Lynch coined the term in 1960. As early as 3000 BCE, Polynesians would read the sun, moon, and stars to gain insights on navigation cues. Even today, knowing that the sun rises in the east and sets in the west, or seeing birds migrate south between the end of August and late October provides navigation cues that make up traditional ideas of wayfinding (Passini 1981; Fewings 2001; Gahbauer 2017). In 300 BCE, wayfinding was developed to create pathways for transport using stone pillars by denoting destinations, distances, and mile markers (Isaak 2018). These physical landmarks paved the way for modern day wayfinding signage on highways that lead to city streets. Within a modern city, outdoor wayfinding includes the presence of residential, commercial, and industrial architectural structures, as well as street signs, street names, addresses, streetlights, railway tracks, tunnels, bridges, and traffic lights. All these components allow individuals to navigate through physical spaces.

Mollerup (2005), a Danish designer and academic, examined it from the other side, coining the term *wayshowing* to describe the various aids or tools that help users carry out the complex task of wayfinding. Wayshowing precedes wayfinding: it examines how institutions and/or organizations can provide support for those users. Wayshowing examples include color-coding signage systems, consistent typefaces, easily accessible maps, and the use of specific shapes, sizes, and colors to denote specific spatial characteristics.

Wayshowing[1] can be divided into two types: architectural wayshowing, which focuses on structures that help a person navigate, and informational wayshowing, which includes signs and maps (Johnston and Mandel 2014). Factors that affect the success of architectural wayshowing include visibility/sightlines, complexity of the physical space, and familiarity, created by reusing the same architectural patterns and settings multiple times. As Mandel (2018) notes, Passini lays out two wayfinding styles that align with these two types: in the spatial style, the user relies on their spatial understanding of the space, which can be supplemented by spatial tools like maps and floor plans. In the linear style, users rely on informational signage to progress from one location to another. Architectural wayshowing systems should be designed by architects, urban planners, and UX designers, with their stakeholders in mind, for while directional and informational signage aids the overall wayfinding system, it cannot always overcome fundamental architectural shortcomings like building complexity or inaccessibility (Arthur and Passini 1992). Existing facilities with architectural design issues should focus on designing effective signage to close the gap (Mandel 2018).

Symonds, Brown and Lo Iacono (2017) assert that wayfinding is an embodied social practice that evokes emotions such as anxiety, joy, nerves, and happiness when moving through a physical space. The authors' conceptual framework comprises the three elements of society, embodied agents, and the environment. The three are connected, as they overlap and work together. The embodied agents are those people with feelings, perceptions, and senses. They interact in buildings with signs, light, technology, and time constraints. They negotiate their practice within society, which comprises power relations, communication tools, capital, and societal norms. For example, persons in positions of power have access to secret and private "backend areas" that separate the haves and have-nots. As written by Goffman (1959), celebrities, professional athletes, royalty, and even office employees are privy to a different embodied experience when they navigate airports, concert halls, sports arenas, and other public facilities shared with the public.

Library Wayfinding

There has been a significant amount of literature about library wayfinding (Johnston and Mandel 2014; Mandel 2009; 2010; 2013; 2017; 2018; Mandel and Johnston 2019; Mandel and LeMeur 2018; Passini 1981). Wayfinding research examines how users navigate through the library environment and discuss the effectiveness of library wayfinding tools (Mandel 2009). Some studies have tracked users' wayfinding paths from the Online Public Access Catalog (OPAC) to the stacks (Eaton 1991). Others have used sketch maps to assess how users navigate through the library's space (Beck 1996). Some write about using ethnographic tools to study wayfinding (Gardner 2018; Horan 1996; Kinsley, Schoonover, and Spitler 2016; Li and Klippel 2012; Schoonover and Kinsley 2014).

Eaton, Vocino, and Taylor (1993) evaluated the impact of directional signage in a confusing, "maze-like" university library on students' library anxiety and overall success in locating the resources that they were seeking. Their study included a short-written questionnaire ($N = 719$) that asked library users to report success or failure in five book searches and to score the perceived helpfulness and usefulness of eight wayfinding aids in the library: signs, labels, directories, you-are-here maps, handheld maps, library staff, other users, and memory of previous visits. The locational aids reported as most helpful were signs (62 percent), memory of past use (84 percent), and labels (52 percent)

(89). The authors also broke down the results according to whether participants were successful and unsuccessful in their five searches. For successful patrons, signs were the most helpful (79 percent), followed by memory (87 percent), and labels (61 percent). Unsuccessful patrons also reported that signs (56 percent) and memory (71 percent) were the most helpful; they ranked library staff as the third most helpful aid (41 percent).

The authors also monitored five selected directional signs, observing each sign five times over a ten-day period. For each observation, the researcher recorded how many people passed and how many stopped to read the sign. They found that directional signs on upper floors were used more than lower-level directional signage: less than 5 percent engaged with lower-level signage, while 19 percent used signage on upper level floors.

Li and Kippel (2012) studied how library architecture affects users' ability to find the resources they are looking for and discovered that signs were very important in assisting participants in their wayfinding. In this study, the authors first used empirical methods to measure the library's visibility, layout complexity, and connectivity. They then observed two groups of participants, one familiar with the library's layout and the other new to the library, asking them to locate two books from each of the library's three towers, then document their journey back to the circulation desk to check out that book. Each participant's wayfinding performance was timed, and the authors found three main criteria affect wayfinding: architectural variation, visibility, and complexity of the physical layout. According to the authors, participants reported that signs were very important in their ability to complete the task.

Wayfinding is made easier by physical clues such as architectural landmarks and variation and layout, but it is also improved by directional signage, display boards, maps, and suspended ceiling signage. It can use color, shape, placement, and the environment to design and develop a system of navigational aids that provide a consistent system for helping users find their way around a physical space.

Facilitating Wayfinding

The International Health Facility Guidelines (2016) establishes the following wayshowing principles:

- Create a unique identity of shapes and colors at each location.
- Give each region a unique visual character.
- Make use of sight lines.
- Create simple, intuitive paths that are easy to navigate.
- Make use of landmarks.

- Avoid information overload.
- Provide signs at decision points.
- Provide wall maps and printed material for users to take.

In interior spaces, particularly those where architectural cues cannot be added or changed, wayfinding designers need to focus on the last three principles, designing wayfinding signage and informational material that help users get from point A to point B. Users need to be able to locate the entrance, exit, emergency exits, stairwells, elevator, restrooms, and permanent physical landmarks (such as beams, columns, a drinking fountain, a staircase, or an elevator) at any time.

Signs can be mounted permanently on walls to become architectural features. These types of permanently affixed signs are difficult to move or remove. Other types of signs may be mounted on walls or ceilings to make them more flexible—able to change as building districts or collections evolve to reflect changing patron needs. Signs can be single or double sided, illuminated, or dynamic. All these types of signs can be helpful in a comprehensive wayshowing system designed to help library users navigate the space.

PLANNING A LIBRARY WAYFINDING SIGNAGE STRATEGY

Below is an overview of the complete process for designing wayfinding signage for your library. Each of these elements will be discussed in detail in further chapters, but this overview can help you choose where your existing wayshowing signage may need updating.

1. Research your audience
2. Analyze the data
3. Develop a wayfinding document that maps out your users' pathways
4. Select decision points
5. Select sign types

   Exterior
   I. Identification (site identification, entrance, exit, parking, accessible parking)
   II. Directional signs

   Interior
   I. Identification (service points, office room numbers, elevators, stairways, restrooms, entrances, and exits)
   II. Directional signs
   III. Orientation (call number ranges, floor directory)
   IV. Regulatory (fire exits, fire alarm pulls)

REFERENCES

Arthur, Paul, and Romedi Passini. 1992. *Wayfinding: People, Signs, and Architecture*. New York: McGraw Hill.

Atkin, Albert. 2010. "Peirce's Theory of Signs." *Mind: A Quarterly Review of Philosophy* 119, no. 475: 852–55.

Barnouw, Jeffrey. 1981. "Signification and Meaning: A Critique of the Saussurean Conception of the Sign." *Comparative Literature Studies* 18, no. 3: 260–71.

Barthes, Roland. 1970. *Empire of Signs*. Translated by Richard Howard. New York: Hill and Wang.

Beck, Susan Gilbert. 1996. "Wayfinding in Libraries." *Library Hi Tech* 14, no. 1: 27–36.

Berger, Craig. 2014. *Typography, Placemaking and Signs: A Four-Part SFI White Paper Series*. Alexandria, VA: Sign Research Foundation. https://signresearch.org/wp-content/uploads/Typography-Placemaking-and-Signs.pdf.

Blades, Mark. 1991. "Wayfinding Theory and Research: The Need for a New Approach." In *Cognitive And Linguistic Aspects of Geographic Space*, 137–65. Dordrecht: Springer.

Bosman, Ellen, and Carol Rusinek. 1997. "Creating the User-Friendly Library by Evaluating Patron Perception of Signage." *Reference Services Review* 25, no. 1: 71–82.

Chandler, Daniel. 2019. "Semiotics for Beginners." July 31, 2019. www.cs.princeton.edu/~chazelle/courses/BIB/semio2.htm.

Dalton, Ruth C., Christoph Holscher, and Daniel R. Montello. 2019. "Wayfinding as a Social Activity." *Frontiers in Psychology* 10, no. 142: 1–14.

Eaton, Gale. 1991. "Wayfinding in the Library: Book Searches and Route Uncertainty." *Reference Quarterly* 30, no. 4: 519–27.

Eaton, Gale, Michael Vocino, and Melanie Taylor. 1993. "Evaluating Signs in a University Library." *Collection Management* 16, no. 3: 81–101.

Eco, Umberto. 1984. *Semiotics and the Philosophy of Language*. Bloomington: Indiana University Press.

Etches, Amanda. 2013. "Know thy Users: User Research Techniques to Build Empathy and Improve Decision-Making." *Reference and User Services Quarterly* 53, no. 1: 13–18.

Fewings, Rodney. 2001. "Wayfinding and Airport Terminal Design." *The Journal of Navigation* 54, no. 2: 177–84.

Gardner, Hollie. 2018. "A User-Centric Approach to Wayfinding Signage." *Public Services Quarterly* 14, no. 4: 373–85.

Giradin, Jean-Claude. 1974. "Toward a Politics of Signs: Reading Baudrillard." *Telos* 1974, no. 20: 127–37.

Goffman, Erving. 1959. *The Presentation of Self in Everyday Life*. New York: Anchor Books.

Hahn, Jim, and Lizz Zitron. 2011. "How First-Year Students Navigate the Stacks." *Reference and User Services Quarterly* 51, no. 1: 28–35.

Hoch, Devon. 2013. "The History of Advertising Signs: Petroglyphs to Present Day." Tex Visions, September 30, 2013. www.texvisions.com/history-of-advertising-signs/.

Horan, Mark. 1999. "What Students See: Sketch Maps as Tools for Assessing Knowledge of Libraries." *The Journal of Academic Librarianship* 25, no. 3: 187–201.

Howe, Nancy, and Wendy Wilsher. 2014. "Creating Clear and Simple Signage." *Library Journal* 139, no. 15: 19–20.

International Health Facility Guidelines. 2016. "Wayfinding Design Principles." In *International Health Facility Guidelines: Part W—Wayfinding Guidelines*. http://healthfacilityguidelines.com/Guidelines/ViewPDF/iHFG/iHFG_part_w_wayfinding_design_principles.

Isaak, Vivian. 2018. "Wayfinding Across Cultures." Magnum Group, April 20, 2018. www.magnumgroupinc.com/wayfinding-across-cultures/.

Jensen, Klaus Bruhn. 2008. "Semiotics." In *The International Encyclopedia of Communication*, edited by Wolfgang Donsbach, 4563–69. Vol. 10. Malden, MA: Blackwell.

Johnston, Melissa P., and Lauren H. Mandel. 2014. "Are We Leaving Them Lost in the Woods with No Breadcrumbs to Follow? Assessing Signage Systems in School Libraries." *School Libraries Worldwide* 20, no. 2: 38–53.

Kinsley, Kirsten M., Dan Schoonover, and Jasmine Spitler. 2016. "GoPro as an Ethnographic Tool: A Wayfinding Study in an Academic Library." *Journal of Access Services* 13, no. 1: 7–23.

Kuhlthau, Carol C. 1991. "Inside the Search Process: Information Seeking from the User's Perspective." *Journal of the American Society for Information Science* 42, no. 5: 361–71.

Kuliga, Saskia F., Benjamin Nelligan, Ruth C. Dalton, Steven Marchette, Amy L. Shelton, Laura Carlson, and Christoph Hölscher. 2019. "Exploring Individual Differences and Building Complexity in Wayfinding: The Case of the Seattle Central Library." *Environment and Behavior* 51, no. 5 : 622–65.

Kupersmith, John. 1987. "Library Anxiety and Library Graphics." *Research Strategies* 5, no. 1: 36–38.

Landis, Mason. 2017. "A Brief History of Modern Signage." Bartush Signs, December 16, 2017. www.bartush.com/history/a-brief-history-of-modern-signage/.

Li, Rui, and Alexander Klippel. 2012. "Wayfinding in Libraries: Can Problems Be Predicted?" *Journal of Map and Geography Libraries* 8, no. 1: 21–38.

Lynch, Kevin. 1960. *The Image of the City*. Vol. 11. Cambridge, MA: MIT Press.

Mackereth, Joseph. 2020. "Wayfinding Is Where Place Meets Information Design." Medium, June 24, 2020. https://medium.com/nightingale/wayfinding-is-where-place-meets-information-design-b668aa224349/.

Mandel, Lauren H. 2009. "Attributing and Defining Meaning to the Built Environment: The Semiotics of Wayfinding." *Proceedings of the American Society for Information Science and Technology* 46, no. 1: 1–6.

Mandel, Lauren H. 2010. "Toward an Understanding of Library Patron Wayfinding: Observing Patrons' Entry Routes in a Public Library." *Library and Information Science Research* 32, no. 2: 116–30.

Mandel, Lauren H. 2012. "Lost in the Labyrinthine Library: A Multi-Method Case Study Investigating Public Library User Wayfinding Behavior." PhD diss. Florida State University.

Mandel, Lauren H. 2013. "Finding Their Way: How Public Library Users Wayfind." *Library and Information Science Research* 35, no. 4: 264–71.

Mandel, Lauren H. 2017. "Wayfinding Research in Library and Information Studies: State of the Field." *Evidence Based Library and Information Practice* 12, no. 2: 133–48.

Mandel, Lauren H. 2018. "Understanding and Describing Users' Wayfinding Behavior in Public Library Facilities." *Journal of Librarianship and Information Science* 50, no. 1: 23–33.

Mandel, Lauren H., and Kelly A. LeMeur. 2018. "User Wayfinding Strategies in Public Library Facilities." *Library and Information Science Research* 40, no. 1: 38–43.

Mandel, Lauren H., and Melissa P. Johnston. 2019. "Evaluating Library Signage: A Systematic Method for Conducting a Library Signage Inventory." *Journal of Librarianship and Information Science* 51, no. 1: 150–61.

Mandel, Lauren H. 2020. "Comparing Different Methodologies Used in Wayfinding Research in Library Facilities." *Qualitative and Quantitative Methods in Libraries* 9, no. 2: 173–90.

Matczak, Jamie. 2018. "Boost! Welcoming, Positive, Consistent Library Signage." *Wisconsin Valley Library Service Newsletter*. www.wvls.org/boost-welcoming-positive-consistent-library-signage/.

Mollerup, Per. 2005. *Wayshowing: A Guide to Environmental Signage: Principles and Practices*. Baden: Lars Müller Publishers.

Passini, Romedi. 1981. "Wayfinding: A Conceptual Framework." *Urban Ecology* 5, no. 1: 17–31.

Petty, Ross D. 2016. "A history of Brand Identity Protection and Brand Marketing." In *The Routledge Companion to Marketing History*, 121–38. Abingdon: Routledge.

Pollet, Dorothy, and Peter C. Haskell. 1979. *Sign Systems for Libraries: Solving the Wayfinding Problem*. New York: Bowker.

Presbrey, Frank. 1929. *History and Development of Advertising*. New York: Doubleday, Doran, and Company.

Samuelson, Robert J. 2000. "The Internet and Gutenberg." *Newsweek (Atlantic Edition)* 135, no. 4: 2.

Samson, Sue, Kim Granath, and Adrienne Alger. 2017. "Journey Mapping the User Experience." *College and Research Libraries* 78, no. 4 : 459–71.

Sassoon, Rosemary, and Albertine Gaur. 1997. *Signs, Symbols and Icons: Pre-History to the Computer Age*. Exeter: Intellect Books.

Schmidt, Aaron, and Amanda Etches. 2014. *Useful, Usable, Desirable*. Chicago: ALA Editions.

Schoonover, Dan, and Kirsten M. Kinsley. 2014. "Stories from the Stacks: Students Lost in the Labyrinth." *Journal of Access Services* 11, no. 3: 175–88.

Symonds, Paul; David H. K. Brown, and Valeria Lo Iacono. 2017. "Wayfinding as an Embodied Sociocultural Experience." *Sociological Research Online* 22, no. 1: 1–20.

Taub, Sarah F. 2001. *Language from the Body: Iconicity and Metaphor in American Sign Language*. Cambridge: Cambridge University Press.

Webster's New World Dictionary. 1970. "Sign." New York: The World Publishing Company.

Zeman, Jay. 1977. "Peirce's Theory of Signs." In *A Perfusion of Signs*, edited by Thomas Sebeok, 22–39. Bloomington: Indiana University Press.

NOTE

1. I use Mollerup's term here for clarity, although the authors mentioned here use the term wayfinding to refer to both the user's process and the institution's tools for enabling that process.

2

Signage Research Methods

THIS CHAPTER DESCRIBES RESEARCH METHODS THAT CAN BE used to study both the efficacy of your library's signage and your users' perceptions and feelings about wayfinding in your library. Most of the research methods here combine traditional social science research methods and user research techniques aligned with UX design and market research, for both wayfinding and UX design study how users navigate through spaces. Most of these research techniques require Institutional Review Board (IRB) approval, especially in academic settings, when the data may be shared or published. You must ensure that your human subjects' privacy is protected, that they are at least eighteen years old, that their responses are either confidential or anonymous, that no physical or emotional distress would be presented to them, that they can withdraw from participating at any time, and that the data will be securely stored and destroyed when the research is completed.

As the previous chapter has shown, wayfinding is a complex subject, and signage is an important part of wayfinding. Signage is particularly important in existing libraries that cannot renovate to increase their architectural wayshowing. It is therefore crucial for libraries to research how users experience their signage practices. This chapter will explain how to conduct user research to understand how your users use your signage, where the signage is effective, and where it fails. Armed with that knowledge, you can audit your signage (chapter 3) to align it with your users' needs and industry best practices.

Mandel (2020) provides a thorough review of twenty-six academic journal articles on wayfinding from library and information science (LIS) journals, comparing the different research methods used. She found that research on library signage and wayfinding used both qualitative and quantitative methods: ethnographic research (interviews, participant observation), experiments, surveys, usability studies, task completion, reflective documentation (journaling, taking photos, video, etc.), and content analysis (signage audits/inventories) were all represented. Mandel confirms that most studies use multiple methods (a combination of quantitative and qualitative), with the most common techniques being interviews, task completion, and observation. However, she found that no method was used consistently across studies because unlike LIS research methods, which are mostly descriptive, library wayfinding research methods are mostly evaluative because they focus on usability and user behavior.

The following section provides an explanation of these various techniques as they are used in signage and wayfinding research.

Ethnographic Research Methods

Ethnographic research, often used by anthropologists, allows researchers to observe a specific group or culture by immersing themselves into that community. Observation is one ethnographic research method that is nonexperimental and qualitative: researchers observe and document participants' actions and behaviors.

There are three types of observational methods in the social sciences: naturalistic, participant, and structured observation. Naturalistic observation can be either disguised or undisguised (Price et al. 2017). Disguised naturalistic observation involves unobtrusively observing participants in their natural environment. Participants should not be aware that researchers are making observations. Some types of naturalistic observation (such as observing individuals' behavior in the restroom) are considered unethical because it violates users' privacy rights (Price et al. 2017). For disguised research techniques to be considered ethical, participants must remain anonymous, and all observations must take place in public settings. In undisguised naturalistic observation, participants are made aware that their behavior is being observed. However, if they know they are being monitored, participants may alter their behavior (Price et al. 2017).

In structured observation, researchers observe a select number of behaviors in a particular setting. This method usually takes place in a controlled environment, such as a laboratory. Researchers are observing naturally occurring behavior, but because of the structured, controlled setting, the data collected is empirical and suited for quantitative analysis (Price et al. 2017).

In participant observation, the researcher is an active participant in the community being studied. This type of observation takes place in a naturalistic setting (Price et al. 2017), and like naturalistic observation above, participant observation can be either *disguised* or *undisguised*. In undisguised participant observation, participants are informed that they are being observed, and this might affect their behavior. In disguised participant observation, the researcher pretends to be part of the group. While this deception is often seen as unethical, it does keep participants from changing their behavior in response to observation (Price et al. 2017).

Two exemplary studies using observation methods are those of Eaton, Vocino, and Taylor (1993) and Mandel (2010). After taking a survey to assess user perceptions of wayfinding signage at a university library, Eaton, Vocino, and Taylor observed five selected signs across four floors of their library. Each of these signs were monitored five times for approximately one hour and forty-five minutes over a ten-day period. The observations confirmed the survey data: fewer than 5 percent of users examined the directional signage for the first two floors, but the floor map signs on the third and fourth floors were used by 19 percent of users (Eaton, Vocino, and Taylor 1993). Similarly, Mandel (2010) covertly observed library patrons' entry routes from two entrances of a medium-sized public library in South Florida. She observed patrons from Monday through Thursday for three time periods of one hour each and three time periods on the weekend, also one hour each, collecting 195 unique routes from 1,415 patrons over the one-week period.

Focus Groups
Focus groups are considered the most time consuming, labor intensive, and costly research methods. They involve facilitated, guided discussions between six and ten people seeking feedback from stakeholders. Generally, focus groups are conducted by one or two researchers who ask semistructured instructions and record (or transcribe) participants' responses. The results may be used for internal purposes (they are often conducted by companies doing market research; Datig 2015; Lotich 2011), or the data may be published. Researchers should ask both structured and open-ended questions, for the open-ended questions often elicit more descriptive, detailed responses.

Audits
Signage audits, discussed in detail in chapter 3, are one of the most thorough self-assessment exercises libraries can carry out. A signage audit involves taking a qualitative and quantitative inventory of all signage, classifying the types of signs, their messages, their design, and their location. Audits attend not only to the number of signs but also to the sign's message, tone, placement, and overall design (colors, composition, images, and branding). Audits ensure that all signs are ADA compliant (see chapter 6) and adhere to commonsense design

practices. Audits are particularly useful in ensuring that patrons do not experience information overload—a common problem with digital signage (discussed in detail in chapter 4), which allows designers to integrate web, audio, video, and social media content into one digital screen. These signs can overload the user to the point of ineffectiveness.

Signage audits should also include other types of user research, such as surveys, focus groups, or interviews, that identify user needs and user perceptions, feelings, and behaviors as they engage with signage. Signage must always be designed with end-user effectiveness in mind. They assess how users experience the library more broadly, evaluating the positivity, usability, and welcoming nature of the library space, including its signage.

Survey Research

Survey research is a method used to collect data from a potential large pool of participants by asking a series of questions, either open-ended or closed. They can be administered through the web (using tools like Surveymonkey or Qualtrics), the telephone (companies often use telephone surveys to gather market research data), or through written questionnaires—one of the most common methods. Surveys collect first-hand data directly from respondents. The US Census is a great example of a large survey. It captures demographic data that helps governments allocate funding to state, regional, and local communities and helps governments plan (if census data from a particular zip code reveals an increase in babies being born, local governments can decide to build more schools, parks, daycares, community health centers, or public library locations). Surveys may pose a variety of different questions. These questions, known as variables, can be of several types, according to Martella et al. (2013). The three types of closed questions most relevant for library research include binary questions (which prompt yes or no answers), nominal questions (which ask the user to classify things into categories), and ordinal (which ask the user to order things by importance).

Interviews and Contextual Inquiry

Interviews, a one-on-one encounter between a researcher and a participant, elicit the richest, most detailed kind of user data (Schmidt and Etches 2014). In *semistructured interviews*, the researcher asks some scripted questions and some unscripted follow-up questions in response to participant answers; these interviews should be informal and conversational in tone, so that participants can freely communicate their opinions, attitudes, and perceptions. These types of interviews usually take place in a space that is separate from the topic of the interview.

Contextual inquiry combines interview questions with observation. In this type of interview, a researcher observes people in their natural environment and asks them questions about tasks they are completing, recording their answers in written field notes or via a recording device (Thornton 2019; Amaresan 2020). Contextual inquiry occurs in the field and the subject has a more active, participatory role. This method is collaborative in nature, as researcher and subject work in tandem.

Interviews and contextual inquiry that are recorded with a digital audio recorder should be transcribed. There are several types of transcription software that can help with this task:

Dragon	Temi
Ebbo	The FTW Transcriber
Express Scribe	Trint
Inqscribe	VoiceRecord Pro
oTranscribe	Wreally

Experiments

According to Martella et al. (2013), experiments are designed to test the causal relationships between two variables. In true experiments, participants are randomly selected and randomly assigned to the treatment and control groups, and both groups are treated equally. In the treatment group, participants are exposed to a change in the independent variable, while the control receives no exposure to change in the independent variable.

There are three types of experiments; pretest-posttest control-group design, posttest-only control-group, and Solomon four-group design. In a pretest-posttest design, the participants are tested before they are exposed to the independent variable, then tested after being exposed. The purpose of this type of experiment is to determine if the manipulating factor (the independent variable) has caused a change in the dependent variable. In posttest-only control groups, the participants in both the treatment group and control group are tested after the treatment group is exposed to the independent variable, allowing researchers to see the effects of the change in the independent variable. The Solomon four-group design is a combination of both of the previous methods: an experiment with the pretest-posttest control group design is run alongside an experiment with the posttest-only control group design. This type of design provides the researcher the most experimental control: it tests both the independent variable's effects and ascertains whether the pretest itself had some effect on the outcome.

An experiment for library signage or wayfinding research would need to take place outside the naturalistic setting of the library itself. In one possible design, the control group could be a random sample of participants who engage with the library's original signage, while the participants in the treatment group could be shown the new signage and asked questions about it. In designing experiments, researchers must avoid the different types of bias, which need not be conscious to have effects on the results (Shuttleworth 2009):

1. Selection/sampling bias: Researchers overrepresent certain groups or omit some groups entirely from samples.
2. Interviewer bias: Researchers ask leading interview questions that solicit specific types of responses from participants.
3. Confirmation bias: Researchers favor responses that confirm a specific point of view or set of beliefs.
4. Measurement bias: Researchers make errors in data collection.
5. Responder bias: Subjects/participants provide responses that they think will satisfy the goals of the researcher.
6. Reporting bias: Researchers report data in ways that support a specific point of view.

Quasi-experiments

Quasi-experiments are research studies that test the causation of a particular phenomenon. However, subjects are not randomly assigned, and the relationship between the variables can thus be explained by multiple hypotheses (Martella et al. 2013). However, it does offer some useful quantitative data that can help drive decision making. Various types of quasi-experiments could be useful and/or accessible to library personnel who are auditing their signage; these are described below.

Eye Tracking

Researchers use eye tracking to study the eye movements of users as they interact with a space. Although this method is usually associated with research into navigation of virtual spaces, such as websites and other graphical user interfaces, eye tracking can be used for physical environments as well. For example, researchers have used eye tracking technology to study drivers' interactions with traffic and road signs and people's navigation through various buildings (hospitals, shopping malls, or public transit centers).

Eye tracking has been traditionally used for educational reasons, particularly for tracking reading behavior, but its use has expanded; now it is used by UX designers, usability researchers, and social media marketers when conducting market research on website usability, social media engagement, and users' interactions with graphic user interfaces (Leggett 2010).

EYE TRACKING SOFTWARE

Farnsworth (2020) provides a selected list of some eye tracking technology (hardware and software) solutions.

Tobii	Oculus
EyeLink	Pupil Labs
SmartEye	Mirametrix
LC Technologies- Eye Gaze device	Ergoneers
	EyeTech
GazePoint	Argus Science

Case Studies

In the social sciences, case studies encompass a specific, detailed examination of a specific library and its specific signage problem. Case studies are self-contained narratives that provide a glimpse into the specific context of that organization. Case studies provide an in-depth understanding of a complex issue in a naturalistic setting. They are exploratory in nature and seek to better understand a phenomenon. Case studies are in stark contrast to experiments because sample selection is not random (like an experiment), and they are studied in naturalistic settings and not a laboratory (Shewan 2018; Crowe et al. 2011).

Case studies are *"slice of life"* observational accounts of an individual, an event, or an organization, offering a specific, detailed examination of a particular phenomenon at a particular site at a particular moment. They are exploratory, naturalistic, and often longitudinal. They are primarily qualitative, but to create this detailed narrative, they may combine multiple data collection techniques, such as interviews, observations, and surveys. Case studies provide a deeper level of analysis that other research methods do not provide. They are not generalizable because sampling is nonrandom, and they do not take place in controlled environments; they therefore cannot be used to explain causality (Price et al. 2017).

In a library, a case study might combine survey research with a few interviews and some observations of users interacting with existing signage to develop a holistic picture of how well your signage is serving your patrons' needs.

Design-Based Research (DBR)

Design-based research (DBR) originates from design science, drawing its roots to product design, artificial intelligence, and aeronautics (Brown 1992; Collins 1992; Collins, Joseph, and Bielaczyc 2004). DBR is a form of participatory research method that involves both researchers and practitioners. It is used primarily in the learning sciences and is concerned with merging theory with practice. It takes place in naturalistic settings, uses mixed methods, and incorporates interventions using an iterative process over a longitudinal period. It is used to inform theoretical knowledge for both researchers and practitioners (Dede 2004). DBR represents a form of experimentation, but takes place in naturalistic settings, as opposed to the controlled setting of a laboratory. DBR uses an iterative process over a lengthy period and compares the results. It is constantly being reworked and improved; thus, this method is in constant evolution. This can be used when signage designers test their sign's effectiveness by assessing both library workers and library users. They may wish to test the effectiveness of a sign's message or placement or design elements.

Participatory Design Research (PDR)

Participatory design research (PDR) is also known as collaborative design, or cooperative design. It involves bringing the participants to the center of the research design (Elizarova, Briselli, and Dowd 2017). The three types of cooperative design may include: designing for participants, designing with participants, and designing by participants (Scariot, Heemann, and Padovani, 2012). PDR extends beyond DBR as a methodology that includes all stakeholders in the research design process. It is collaborative and includes the voices of all contributors to the research experiment. It takes into account all participants who are involved in the research. This method is more innovative and inclusive as it includes more voices and points of view. This inclusive practice leads to a more democratic and equitable design that helps promote transformative social change (Bang and Vossoughi 2016). Researchers recruit participants for this study who will play a participatory role. The subjects of the study are stakeholders who play an active role in the study. This may present issues such as selection bias to the research design. Unlike traditional studies, researchers are not directing the subjects; they play a central role and are at the center of the study. PDR is often associated with ethnographic research, a method that is not perceived as generalizable. Because PDR is qualitative in nature, the results will be more descriptive and detailed and provide rich insights to the researcher.

User Experience (UX) Mapping

UX mapping is a research method that is used in UX research. It tracks the pathways that users take as they move through the library facility to perform a particular task, such as locating books in the stacks or finding the silent study area of the library. To implement this method, participants chronicle their journey through the library using graphical means. Some UX maps are technical, asking users to document the paths they took to get from point A to point B; these maps shed light on your building's particular idiosyncrasies, identifying touch points where library users make decisions and informing library workers about where signage would help users navigate. Other maps are descriptive, asking users to document their feelings and emotions as they navigate through virtual and physical spaces. Types of mapping that could be useful for a library signage audit include journey mapping, empathy mapping, experience mapping, and service mapping (Gibbons 2017).

Journey mapping provides insight into the different ways library users navigate within the facility. A journey map includes five components: (1) persona (a profile of a fictional individual profile of a user group), (2) the scenario, (3) the stages (or phases) of the journey, (4) the actions and emotions, and (5) the insights that the person gleaned from the journey (Gibbons 2018). A more abbreviated journey map can include three components: (1) the touchpoints, (2) the stages, and (3) the notes from the actual journey (Marquez, Downey, and Clement 2015). In a journey map, the user is given a scenario (or task) that they must complete, and they produce a visual narrative of the journey they took to complete the task. The map includes the scenario, the expected journey, the user's actual journey (or steps), their "pain points" (or obstacles), their reflections (successful and unsuccessful transactions), and their recommendations for improvement (Samson, Granath, and Alger 2017). A more abbreviated journey map can focus simply on three core components: (1) the touchpoints, (2) the stages, and (3) the notes from the actual journey (Marquez, Downey, and Clement 2015).

Empathy mapping can help understand the user's mindset when they are confronted with specific signs. These maps ask participants to record their reactions on a map divided into four quadrants: *says, thinks, feels,* and *does*. The user is asked to document their questions that relate to the four domains. For example, in an empathy map studying library signage, in the *says* quadrant, the user would record what the sign is saying to them—its overt message. In the *thinks* quadrant, the user is asked to document what they think about the sign's intended message. For *feels*, the user is asked to jot down the feelings they experience when engaging with the sign, and in the *does* quadrant, the user records how they reacted—what they did in response to the sign.

Experience mapping is used before a user is asked to create a journey map; it maps the general behavior of "the user"—a generic person rather than an individual user, as with a journey map. Like empathy maps, it examines phases, actions, thoughts, and mindsets/emotions. This method is often used when conducting market research to gain an understanding of a particular user group. Experience mapping is often used to inform or predict the results of particular users' journey maps (Gibbons 2017).

Service mapping (or service blueprinting) is a form of self-assessment aimed at identifying weaknesses across an entire set of organizational processes, including customer actions, front-stage interactions, backstage interactions, support processes, physical evidence, inventory, and line of visibility (Gibbons 2017). This type of self-assessment mapping takes place after user journey mapping and is informed by the experiences documented in those journey maps. It assesses the relationships between different service points or touchpoints in an organization, visualizing organizational processes to streamline organizational efficiency. In a library signage audit, this map might examine how library signs are connected to a specific service or resource and how they might better convey necessary information to improve users' experiences in accessing that service or resource.

Cultural Probes (Reflective Documentation)
Cultural probes (also known as diary studies) are an ethnographic research technique in which participants record their observations, take photographs, compose diary entries, and produce video (using tools supplied to them by researchers) to articulate their experiences navigating through the built environment. This method can be applied to UX design and library wayfinding research (Datig 2015; Schmidt and Etches 2014; Murphy 2006). While it collects rich data, the data is narrow and not generalizable, for it records only the experience of a single person; therefore, this method is often triangulated with other research techniques, such as focus groups (Murphy 2006).

A/B Testing
A/B testing is a very straightforward user research technique, in which participants are asked to compare two slightly different versions of the same content. One version is the control group (which remains unchanged) and the other version has a slight variation. Participants are tested and asked which version they prefer. This technique is usually associated with website usability studies, but it can also be used for comparative studies of signage design.

Task Completion
Task completion, which comes from UX research, can be used in library wayfinding studies. One example of task completion is the card sorting method. Participants are given various flash cards and are asked to organize them into categories. Card sorting is often used in website usability studies to inform the website menu structure, information architecture, or website navigation (Mandel 2020; Schmidt and Etches 2014); in the context of library signage, participants might be asked to classify signage into different categories. Another form of task completion is the think-aloud method, where users record themselves verbally articulating their experiences as they navigate through the library's physical space. The task is to complete a journey to find a particular book or meeting room;

this qualitative method can thus help signage and wayfinding designers better understand users' experiences as they move from point A to point B (Datig 2015; Mandel 2020; Kinsley, Schoonover, and Spitler 2016).

Usability Testing

Usability testing involves asking users to perform a series of tasks and then observing their behavior. Insights from participants' actions can help improve service by shedding light on the problems users encounter in accessing specific products or services. There are three types of usability testing: moderated, unmoderated, and guerilla. Moderated usability tests are usually held in person or live via online screensharing tools. An unbiased facilitator or researcher asks the participant to complete a series of tasks (and sometimes to think aloud while doing so) while stakeholders observe the process through a one-way mirror or through screensharing. In unmoderated usability tests, the participant records themselves performing the tasks and sends their completed documentation of their tasks to the researcher; the observers watch the recording of the task completion after the fact. Guerilla testing is similar to moderated usability testing, but it's conducted in the field, in a naturalistic setting where many potential users may wish to participate (Moran 2019).

Cognitive Mapping

Cognitive mapping allows users to create a visual representation of their mental model of a particular phenomenon, allowing users to mentally brainstorm concepts and make connections between them. This type of user research is exploratory and unstructured. Signage researchers may employ this method to help develop the language for their signs. A cognitive mapping session would typically involve an interview that is partly improvised and partly structured. An ice breaker or trigger question is used to start the interview. A potential question might be:

> When I say the words, "friendly and welcoming sign that asks users to not use their cell phones in the library," what are some of the first words that come to mind? Please think out loud and write down each word that comes to mind on the flipchart (or notebook).

The user interview can be a single session or can be multiple sessions in length. Throughout the interview, the three assessments that are collected are the (1) transcript of the interview (or recorded video), (2) the map created by the participant, and (3) the researcher's field notes (Gibbons 2019).

User Research Software Solutions

Various proprietary software packages provide access to different tools for user research. Some provide templates that implement and manage user surveys, journey maps, interviews, cultural probes (diaries), usability tests, A/B testing, focus groups, task completions, and audio/video transcriptions. Others can manage a database of participants, pay incentives, recruit potential participants, and automate research activities for researchers. The following is a selected list of user research software solutions:

Airtable	LookBack	TestingTime
Dragon Naturally Speaking	Maze	TypeForm
	Optimal Workshop	UsabilityHub
Dscout	QuestionPro	Usabilla
EnjoyHQ	Reduct Video	User Interviews
Ethnio	Reframer	User Testing
Evolt	Respondent	UserVoice
GoTranscript	Survey Monkey	UserZoom
LimeSurvey	Qualtrics	

REFERENCES

Amaresan, Swetha. 2020. "The Expert's Guide to Contextual Inquiry Interviews." Hubspot blog, May 5, 2020. https://blog.hubspot.com/service/contextual-inquiry/.

Bang, Megan, and Shirin Vossoughi. 2016. "Participatory Design Research and Educational Justice: Studying Learning and Relations within Social Change Making." *Cognition and Instruction* 34, no. 3: 173–93.

Brown, Ann L. 1992. "Design Experiments: Theoretical and Methodological Challenges in Creating Complex Interventions in Classroom Settings." *Journal of the Learning Sciences* 2, no. 2: 141–78.

Collins, Allan. 1992. "Toward a Design Science of Education." In *New Directions in Educational Technology*, 15–22. Berlin: Springer.

Collins, Allan, Diana Joseph, and Katerine Bielaczyc. 2004. "Design Research: Theoretical and Methodological Issues." *Journal of the Learning Sciences* 13, no. 1: 15–42.

Crowe, Sarah, Kathrin Cresswell, Ann Robertson, Guro Huby, Anthony Avery, and Aziz Sheikh. 2011. "The Case Study Approach." *BMC Medical Research Methodology* 11, no. 1: 1–9.

Datig, Ilka. 2015. "Walking in Your Users' Shoes: An Introduction to User Experience Research as a Tool for Developing User-Centered Libraries." *College and Undergraduate Libraries* 22, no. 3–4: 234–46.

Dede, Chris. 2004. "If Design-Based Research Is the Answer, What Is the Question? A Commentary on Collins, Joseph, and Bielaczyc; diSessa and Cobb; and Fishman, Marx, Blumenthal, Krajcik, and Soloway in the JLS Special Issue on Design-Based Research." *Journal of the Learning Sciences* 13, no. 1: 105–14.

Eaton, Gale, Michael Vocino, and Melanie Taylor. 1993. "Evaluating Signs in a University Library." *Collection Management* 16, no. 3: 81–101.

Elizarova, Olga, Jen Briselli, and Kimberly Dowd. 2017. "Participatory Design: What It Is, What It Isn't, and How It Actually Works." December 14, 2017. *UX Magazine*, article 1695: 14. https://uxmag.com/articles/participatory-design-in-practice/.

Farnsworth, Bryn. 2020. "Top 12 Eye Tracking Hardware Companies (Ranked)." IMotions blog, March 3, 2020. https://imotions.com/blog/top-eye-tracking-hardware-companies/.

Gibbons, Sarah. 2017. "UX Mapping Methods Compared: A Cheat Sheet." Nielsen Norman Group, November 5, 2017. https://www.nngroup.com/articles/ux-mapping-cheat-sheet/.

———. 2018. "Journey Mapping 101." Nielsen Norman Group, December 9, 2018. www.nngroup.com/articles/journey-mapping-101/.

———. 2019. "Cognitive Mapping in User Research." Nielsen Norman Group, August 11, 2019. www.nngroup.com/articles/cognitive-mapping-user-research/.

Kinsley, Kirsten M., Dan Schoonover, and Jasmine Spitler. 2016. "GoPro as an Ethnographic Tool: A Wayfinding Study in an Academic Library." *Journal of Access Services* 13, no. 1: 7–23.

Leggett, David. 2010. "A Brief History of Eye-Tracking." UX Booth, January 19, 2010. www.uxbooth.com/articles/a-brief-history-of-eye-tracking/.

Lotich, Patricia. 2011. "What Is the Purpose and Advantages of Focus Group Interviews?" *Social Media Today*, August 16, 2011. www.socialmediatoday.com/content/what-purpose-and-advantages-focus-group-interviews/.

Mandel, Lauren H. 2010. "Toward an Understanding of Library Patron Wayfinding: Observing Patrons' Entry Routes in a Public Library." *Library and Information Science Research* 32, no. 2: 116–30.

Mandel, Lauren H. 2020. "Comparing Different Methodologies Used in Wayfinding Research in Library Facilities." *Qualitative and Quantitative Methods in Libraries* 9, no. 2: 173–90.

Marquez, Joe J., Annie Downey, and Ryan Clement. 2015. "Walking a Mile in the User's Shoes: Customer Journey Mapping as a Method to Understanding the User Experience." *Internet Reference Services Quarterly* 20, no. 3–4: 135–50.

Martella, Ronald C., J. Ron Nelson, Robert L. Morgan, and Nancy E. Marchand-Martella. 2013. *Understanding and Interpreting Educational Research*. New York: Guilford Press.

Moran, Kate. 2019. "Usability Testing 101." Nielsen Norman Group, December 1, 2019. www.nngroup.com/articles/usability-testing-101/.

Murphy, John. 2006. "Cultural Probes: Understanding Users in Context." *User Experience Magazine*, September 2006. https://uxpamagazine.org/cultural_probes/.

Price, Paul C., Rajiv Jhangiani, I-Chant A. Chiang, Dana C. Leighton, and Carrie Cuttler. 2017. *Research Methods in Psychology*. Montreal: Pressbooks. https://opentext.wsu.edu/carriecuttler/.

Samson, Sue, Kim Granath, and Adrienne Alger. 2017. "Journey Mapping the User Experience." *College and Research Libraries* 78, no. 4: 459–71.

Scariot, Cristiele A., Adriano Heemann, and Stephania Padovani. 2012. "Understanding the Collaborative-Participatory Design." *Work* 41, no. 1: 2701–5.

Shewan, Dan. 2018. "How to Write a Convincing Case Study in 7 Steps." WordStream blog, April 30, 2018. www.wordstream.com/blog/ws/2017/04/03/how-to-write-a-case-study/.

Shuttleworth, Martyn. 2009. "Research Bias." Explorable, February 9, 2009. https://explorable.com/research-bias/.

Thornton, Patrick. 2019. "Go Beyond User Interviews with Contextual Inquiry." UX Collective, March 5, 2019. https://uxdesign.cc/contextual-inquiry-a-primer-14e2e0696fb9/.

3
Conducting a Signage Audit

SIGNS ARE LIVING DOCUMENTS, AND THEY NEED TO BE REVIS-ited and revised on a regular basis. Your library's existing signage should undergo a periodic signage audit to critically evaluate the signs' intended message, design, purpose, and placement. Signage audits let you take ownership of your library's message. They provide a clean slate, allowing you to revise your communication strategy by updating language, images, policies, branding, and placement.

Published Literature on Library Signage Audits

This section reviews literature on libraries that have done signage audits, reporting their processes, findings, and best practices. This chapter also provides *before* and *after* photographs of these libraries' signage.

Johnston and Mandel (2014) wrote about their pilot study where they analyzed 435 signs in three different school libraries (elementary school, middle school, and high school). Their central argument is that school library signage must be an effective wayfinding aid because wayfinding is directly related to spatial literacy, which are crucial for school-aged children. They cite many other studies that report a lack of directional signage in libraries. The authors categorized the signs audited into three categories: informational (83 percent), policy (14.7 percent), and directional (2.3 percent). They identified eight issues (or problems) relating to these signs: wrong location, unclear, poor use of color, placement, not current, damaged sign, and damaged holder. (These eight problems are further discussed in chapter 5.)

Mandel and Johnston (2019) wrote about an extensive signage audit of three school libraries, one public library, and one academic library, undertaken to determine the optimal amount and type of signage for libraries. They cite multiple studies showing that libraries often contain either too much or too little signage. They used a coding reference sheet to record the total number of signs and applied a formula to determine whether there were too few or too many. They took photographs of both problem signs and good signs, and their inventory for each library labeled each of the signs, categorized them, described each one's size, location in the space, specific placement, language, and identifiable problems.

Stempler and Polger (2013) and Polger and Stempler (2014) wrote about a multiyear library signage audit and replacement project they undertook at the College of Staten Island, one of the twenty-five campuses of the City University of New York (CUNY). Their audit involved counting the number of signs on each floor of the library, sorting the signs into different categories, identifying the signs' problems, and developing a replacement strategy. Their audit was a complete overhaul: based on data from a staff and student survey with A/B testing of different signage designs and messages, they created a signage policy that addressed messaging, design, branding, placement, location, size, typeface, color scheme, and ADA compliance.

Warren and Epp (2016) conducted a "kindness" signage audit that examined space, usability, and signage over the twenty locations in the University of Manitoba library system. This study focuses on UX in relation to signage and wayfinding. This kindness audit focused on library space, evaluating how welcoming and user-friendly the environments were. (Library kindness audits were originally introduced by Olin and Hardenbrook [2015] at the ACRL national virtual conference. This original kindness audit addressed furniture, signage, seating, study space, cleanliness, lighting, sound issues, and other characteristics of the physical space, describing what characteristics library users liked and what they disliked.)

Luca and Narayan (2016) conducted a signage audit based on UX design principles. Their signage audit revealed that they had too many signs, inconsistent branding, too much text, and information overload. In addition, many signs were in poor condition—faded, untidy, and old. Their audit used a participatory design methodology known as design thinking. Design thinking comes from design science, or the science of product design. It involves creating prototypes, gathering feedback, collaborating with subjects (participants), and making many iterations. Design thinking is loosely related to design-based research, a methodology from the learning sciences that involves an iterative process of interventions. In terms of library signage, designers would use these iterative processes of feedback and implementation as they assess how library users respond to signage (Bowler and Large 2008). Luca and Narayan took an inventory, photographing each sign, annotating the photograph, entering it in a spreadsheet, and classifying it into various categories based on their purpose. Each sign was evaluated based on its usefulness, intended purpose, and clarity. The spreadsheet included a column indicating whether the sign should be removed or updated and whether the new logo should be added to the updated sign.

Schmidt (2015) and Matczak (2018) both write about the importance in creating welcoming, user-friendly signs that have a consistent typeface and logo and that contain positive language. Roberts (2005) argued that positive language makes library signage more welcoming to patrons, and White (2010), Serfass (2012), Schmidt (2015), and Kasperek (2014) assert that negative messaging in signage should be removed altogether. They offer guidelines such as avoiding library jargon, ensuring signs are readable from a distance, placing them at an appropriate height, and using images that reflect the diversity of the library's user base.

Bosman and Rusinek (1997) conducted a signage inventory by annotating over 200 signs, documenting their size, shape, color, format, message, and purpose (directional, informational, or instructional). The authors excluded signs for restrooms, call number signage, and backlit signs. They photographed all signs, service points, and hallways to evaluate existing signs' placement. They also distributed two surveys over a two-year period (pre- and posttest—before and after the changes to the library's signs) to assess patron perceptions of the signage before and after the inventory and replacement. These surveys were randomly distributed to 10 percent of the student population; 421 students responded to the first survey and 317 responded to the follow-up survey. The short survey asked two questions about how the respondent used the library and how many times per week they visited it. The remaining five questions were Likert scale questions about the signage. Two questions asked users to respond to their understanding of two sets of signs: three policy signs and two instructional signs. Two more questions asked how useful the signage was for wayfinding: one asked about locating specific library service points (reference desk, circulation desk, archives, government documents, elevators, stairs, fire exists, and restrooms) and one asked about locating books using call number signage. The last question asked about user's overall level of difficulty in using all library signage. The authors also detailed the process of creating a replacement plan. A signage vendor estimated a cost of $25,000 (in 1994) to replace all signs in the library. The authors chose to prioritize directional signage—a particular weak spot, as only 1 percent of the original signs had been directional—and simply removed all handwritten signs (40 percent of the original signage!). In the end, they spent $5,000 for the professional signage replacement.

Audit from the Point of View of User Experience (UX)

UX relates to the overall emotional experience when a user interacts with a physical or virtual space. One way to ensure that user needs and user emotional experiences are at the center of library design choices is to do a signage audit from the point of view of the user. This section offers an overview of UX design and how these standards and principles apply to the design of signage, which should support its purpose and message. UX design sheds light on how users perceive your physical and virtual spaces, and how they feel during interactions with those spaces. This information should drive your signage audit, for the purpose of the audit is to design signage that meets users'—not library workers'—needs.

In a library setting, UX has to do with the overall design of the library's physical spaces: doorways, entrances and exits, restrooms, furniture, the orientation of the circulation and reference desk, the display cases, and all of the signage. Many scholars have argued that physical elements of the library should be designed with user experience in mind.[1] While UX also applies to virtual spaces (such as library websites and user interfaces on various library databases, such as the library catalog or periodical databases), there is a tremendous amount of existing library literature devoted to UX design for these virtual spaces,[2] while there is very little information available applying these principles to library signage. Therefore, I focus here on how to design your signage using UX design concepts in this chapter to reduce users' anxiety and confusion and increase their positive feelings and experiences as they navigate your library.

What Is Good UX for Signage?

According to Schmidt and Etches (2014), the three key qualities that make up good UX are (1) *usability,* (2) *usefulness,* and (3) *desirability.* When it comes to library signage, the sign must solve a problem (usefulness), satisfy a need (usability), and serve a purpose (desirability).

Usability relates to the sign's understandability and ease-of-use in both its language and its design. According to Jakob Nielsen (2012), the usability of a sign can be judged using five criteria: learnability, efficiency, memorability, errors, and satisfaction. In terms of library signage, *learnability* has to do with how easy users find it to understand a sign's meaning; *efficiency* relates to on how quickly users can respond to the sign; *memorability* captures how well users can recall the sign's message; *errors* measure the sign's effectiveness via its "rejection rate" of how often users reject the sign's message; and *satisfaction* refers to the user's feelings, positive or negative, when they interact with that sign.

Usefulness is the combination of *usability* and *utility* (Nielsen 2012). It measures how necessary the sign is; a useful sign must have a purpose—promotional, policy, or directional. *Utility* is about satisfying a user's goals and objectives in completing a task (Thornton 2019), and is thus centered on the user's needs and values. To have utility to a user, the sign must solve a problem for them and meet their need.

Desirability is the level of intensity of the user need that the sign meets. Some of the most asked questions at the reference desk include: How do I locate a textbook? Where are the restrooms? What are your hours? How do I reset my password? This information is highly desirable; library users need and want this information. Signs that answer these questions are considered useful and desirable and should be designed to be sure that they are also usable.

User-Centered Design for Wayfinding

In a library environment, users engage via different channels (or pathways), each of which directs them to a different library service point: circulation, reference, the classroom, media services, interlibrary loan, printer, scanners, and photocopy machines. Thinking from the perspective of the user, we can see the library as a large, interconnected web of these service points woven together. Library users move across different channels that use various library services. These services should work together and provide a cohesive and interconnected experience that is seamless and user friendly (Marquez, Downey, and Clement 2015). The same is true for virtual library environments: individuals access a library website and navigate through the website through different paths, in the same way that they travel through library buildings. Online tools such as Google Analytics can help website designers by providing data on how users access websites, where they come from, the time of day, how they arrive on the various web pages, how long they stay on the page, and their route.

If the physical space makes a person disoriented, it increases their anxiety and distress. This is especially relevant in the library, where users are particularly anxious about many tasks: navigating the physical facility, conducting research, browsing the stacks, or finding information on the library website.

Principles of good UX design for wayfinding ensure that users can understand the relationships between spaces and identify the purpose of these spaces. An effective wayfinding system allows users to circulate within space without getting lost. When designing spaces in built environments, there are several wayfinding principles that need to be considered.[3]

- Create spaces that are intuitive and not confusing.
- Provide only relevant, necessary information for the user.
- Remove unnecessary elements to provide clear, unobstructed views ahead.
- Use sight lines to show what is ahead.
- Create clear touch points with signs that offer the users decisions.
- Use landmarks and wall maps to aid users in navigating the space.
- Create zones with unique identities.
- Create and define natural paths for users to navigate.
- Incorporate appropriate touchpoints where pathways branch out.

Wayfinding systems should inform users of the appropriate path(s) in built environments. They should confirm the correct start and finish points of the user's journey, and they should offer a you-are-here confirmation at each touch point to reinforce that they are traveling in the right direction, increasing user confidence.

User emotions are at the heart of user centered and UX design, including signage design more broadly and wayfinding signage design specifically. Symonds, Brown, and Lo Iacono (2017) argue that wayfinding is an embodied social activity, yet in their review of wayfinding literature, they find that the *body* has been missing. Wayfinding, they argue, is an experience where bodies interact with each other and with the physical environment.

UX principles should be applied when creating new print and digital signage in library spaces in ways that consider the emotional well-being of the user. Below are some reflective questions to ask yourself during the design process.

- How can I create signage that is concise and clear?
- How can I create signage that is not confusing?
- How will this sign make them feel?
- How can I be friendly?
- How can I make a sign that is welcoming?
- How can this sign be interpreted in a way (that I did not intend)?
- How can I avoid being passive aggressive or sarcastic?

UX design is about getting inside the mind of your users. As Etches (2013) puts it, UX design is about showing empathy and by putting yourself in your user's shoes. She states that "user research data elevates the discussion based on staff opinion to actual behavior of the people you serve" (14). Library workers think they know their users, and their intentions are always good, but if they don't utilize tools that get into the mindset of the user (such as user research), then they will waste time without satisfying the user's needs and expectations.

Performing Your Own Signage Audit

A signage audit comprises four main phases: the inventory of the existing signage system, the classification of existing signs, user research (on what areas need more or different signage; on existing signs' utility; or on proposed replacement signage), and the redesign and replacement of signs. Sometimes there is an additional user research phase to test proposed sign design during or after this phrase. Kupersmith (1980) identified five phases of a signage design project: (1) research/analysis, (2) schematic design, (3) design development, (4) installation, and (5) maintenance. Sufficient time should be spent on the planning and classification of the types of signs to be produced, along with an evaluation of user needs, the number of signs, and their locations. He argues that during the five phases, continuous evaluation should take place throughout the project. To maintain effectiveness, he recommends preparing guidelines so that library signage remains unified and consistent in design and messaging, conducting systematic research on how to maintain effectiveness (see chapter 2), peruse library literature, and examine case studies from other libraries; librarians should collaborate with designers and foster communication on signage best practices, and have staff-in by thinking of library signage as instructional in nature.

Inventory

Most library signage inventory projects are aimed at keeping existing signage up to date, ensuring that it is current, relevant, and reflects an accurate snapshot of the current physical and virtual library space.[4] First, library workers must know the current state of the existing signage. A signage inventory documents the number and location of each sign, along with its physical condition, size, color, shape, and type/purpose. Inventories may also include photographs of existing signs.

Categorization and Assessment

This phase is one of the most important steps in a signage audit; it involves classifying signs into different categories, using both quantitative and qualitative assessment. Many authors describe this phase as organizing their signage based on type, size, color, message, shape, and location. Most literature written about library signage redesign projects separate signage into three categories: informational, policy, and directional. Others add additional categories, such as identification, promotional, and instructional signage.

In their categorization phase, Mandel and Johnston (2019) identified not only the basics (type of sign, size, and location) but also any problems associated with that sign, such as physical damage (including vandalism), outdatedness, or inefficient or unwelcoming messaging (messaging that is punitive, off-brand, confusing, or inconsistent). In this phase, it is wise to develop a thesaurus, compiling the language used in the signs to create consistency (Polger 2014). Signage auditors can also document signage locations by photographing signs or sketching a signage locator map (Polger and Stempler 2014).

User Research
After the comprehensive signage inventory and preliminary assessment, the audit should move into the user research phase. In this phase, you learn how signage can be improved, replaced, or removed to better serve patrons' needs. This phase employs the many different research techniques that study user behavior, attitudes, perceptions, and feelings. These techniques (many of which come from market research) were described in detail in chapter 2. User research allows library workers to get inside the user's head (and shoes) to better understand how they think and how they use the library's physical and virtual spaces.

Removal and Replacement
The last phase is the actual removal and replacement of signs. It involves not only removing and replacing signs but also documenting the quantity and type of sign posted, their placements, their locations, and their purposes. This might be the most rewarding stage of a signage audit, especially if the original signage was physically damaged, contained an outdated brand or logo, or was punitive, unclear, passive aggressive, confusing, text-heavy, or contradictory. Very often, libraries have far more signs than they need, so after replacement, the library may have fewer signs than before the audit.

Maintenance
Even after replacement, signs must be assessed and evaluated on a regular basis because they are living documents. Periodically revisit signs and examine their physical condition, placement, size, ADA compliancy, location, message, purpose, and overall style with an eye to potential updates. Similarly, library workers should regularly observe users interacting with signs and the navigational pathways they follow, ensuring that the signs are placed along visible sightlines and at the touchpoints where users make navigational decisions. Library workers should also attend to where and when users ask directional or informational questions; reference librarians (who are often the most visible, accessible workers in a library and thus field the bulk of these questions) might keep a log of

these types of directional questions to help with the ongoing project of signage maintenance.

Library signage, like libraries themselves, are living entities. In other words, a pristine, perfectly organized library is an unused, *dead space*. Libraries are meant to be in disruptive states of chaos, which signals that they are being used to find information, study, collaborate, socialize, and participate in community.

Signage Audit Case Studies

Below are some short case studies from different libraries that describe their library's signage audit and the reasons why they needed to update their signage. Each summary has been written by different contributors from various public and academic library.

SAN DIEGO UNIVERSITY LIBRARY
Sallee Spearman, Director of Budget and Fiscal Operations

San Diego State University (SDSU) Library recently revised wayfinding signage panels on all the floors of the 500,000 square foot Malcolm E. Love Library. Opened in 1971, the building is undergoing a phased renovation. During the last two years, unit and collection relocations made it necessary to change the existing signage, and more changes are yet to come. While the university intends to support permanent signage, the library's need was immediate.

While SDSU has an excellent graphic design program, we hired a student assistant to work part-time on temporary signage. A member of staff in a communications/PR position supervised the student's work. A librarian and a public desk lead provided feedback. A newly hired graphic designer provided design input. We instituted a phased try-it-and-see approach. Starting with small projects, the knowledge gained informed subsequent work. The most recent phase created fifteen unique floor-to-ceiling adhesive wall panels for Love Library, complete with directional arrows, colored guides for resources and collections, and you-are-here maps.

An earlier UX committee determined that poor wayfinding was undermining resource discovery. At that time, students would consult emergency evacuation maps for wayfinding help; getting lost in Love Library was almost a rite of passage. Thanks to the latest iteration of signage, those days are behind us. We now have control over the design of our signs and can update as needed. Interim dean, Patrick McCarthy believes the signage will have "a significant impact on a student's ability to navigate the library." The investment was definitely worthwhile.

The Malcolm E. Love Library at San Diego State is comprised of over 300,000 square feet on five floors. Elevator and stair access is located in a central core. The interiors of the upper three floors are almost identical, creating a very confusing situation for patrons. The wayfinding project was limited in scope and could not include painting or flooring changes. It focused solely on updating existing panels at the stair and elevator entrance/egress points. The existing sign panels were out-of-date and incorrect; they were a dark color with poor contrast; and they provided only the most rudimentary content (location and arrows).

BEFORE   AFTER

CONDUCTING A SIGNAGE AUDIT | 39

RIVIER UNIVERSITY LIBRARY
Kathleen MacFarline, Research & Instruction Librarian

Don't Reshelve Magazines

BEFORE

AFTER

The original version of this sign stood out with its nineties-style clip art and font, and sounded like it was giving orders more than asking. We softened the wording and included an explanation as to *why* they were being asked to do this, as well as updating the illustration to a more modern look.

Educational Resource Center (ERC)

BEFORE

AFTER

Stacks Signage

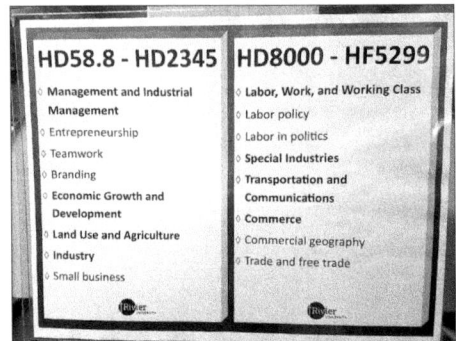

BEFORE   AFTER

Our original stacks signs served their purpose, but we wanted to make it easier for students to browse if they wound up in the stacks without a call number in hand. We also thought there were a lot of them that highlighted super-obscure sections of the LC Classification System that our students were unlikely to be looking for. Our first step was revisiting which topics and subjects we were including on the signs.

After doing some research and investigating several libraries' best practices for stacks signage, we were highly impressed with the University of Technology Sydney's design, so we used that as a jumping-off point for our own. Where they had two individual signs for the end of an aisle, we combined that into one. And while they used a long multicolored "ribbon" to represent all the different areas of their collection, we limited ours to three colors—one for each floor. We also added text to the bottom of the sign encouraging patrons to reach out if they need help.

We wanted the colors to pop and ended up with brighter variations of some of the brand colors from our university website. We extended this color-coding throughout the floor, including the smaller call number range signs on the end caps.

Other Signage

In the course of our signage audit, we came across two different signs for the bins of papers that had been left on the library printers. We decided to consolidate these into a single design for use across the building. Both of the previous signs featured clip art, and the first was hanging on by a few visible pieces of tape. The second used everyone's favorite font, Comic Sans, and included a "Call for Papers" academic reference that the average undergraduate probably wouldn't understand. We modernized the sign with an updated graphic and fonts, and printed it on cardstock to keep it standing straighter.

MARTIN LUTHER COLLEGE
Linda Kramer, Director of Library Services

In 2018, the main level of our library received a facelift with new carpet and paint. During this time, we also rearranged shelving and furniture and attempted to make our library look its best. In this process, we realized that we had forty-plus kinds of signs and labels, and no wayfinding signage except a building map posted by the front desk.

For wayfinding, we used the same style as is being used in other buildings because our campus is gradually improving its overall wayfinding signage. This incorporates the school colors of black, white, and red. We felt that this was a way of making the library feel like a part of the overall campus rather than a big, separate building.

We designed a consistent style for our other signs and labels, using a template with a few variations so we can add other signs as needed. We also used this style on our campus-wide digital signage in an attempt to make people think "library" when they see this style of sign. It also makes it quicker and simpler to make new signs because we can just plug the information into a template. We feel that the look of the library has improved and are happy with the changes that have been made.

BEFORE **AFTER**

WILMINGTON MEMORIAL LIBRARY
Tina Stewart, Library Director

Spurred by the loss of funding for a new building in 2005, and with inspiration from the 2006 PLA Conference in Boston, the Wilmington Memorial Library (WML) staff committed itself to making over the 15,000 square foot library, transforming it from a dated building with challenging space constraints into an inviting and welcoming facility.

The makeover included adding flexible furnishings and more display space. Slatwall end panels were added to the book stacks and the nonfiction collection was reorganized into "neighborhoods." New signage was created to guide patrons to the new organization of these collections. The new sign system is used throughout the building.

The signs are created using Adobe InDesign and sent to GotPrint, the online printing company that we use. We purchased the plexiglass sign holders from Gaylord. This signage system is inexpensive and allows us to easily change the signs if needed at minimal cost.

We also "cleaned up" our bulletin boards by purchasing slatwalls and plexiglass sign holders for our program flyers. The program flyers that are created follow the library's style guide which was created in 2011.

BEFORE

AFTER

BOOTH LIBRARY, EASTERN ILLINOIS UNIVERSITY
Elizabeth Heldebrandt, Public Relations Director

Booth Library was built in 1948–50. The building was expanded in 1968. In 1998, a complete renovation was undertaken, and the building reopened in 2002. The renovation was very attractive and award-winning. Given the beauty of the library, it was decided no signage would be posted as it would reduce the eye-pleasing aesthetics, and most patrons would ask at the public service desks if they were unable to locate what they needed.

In August of 2018, a new dean was appointed. During one of the first all-library employee meetings, a question of signage in the library was brought up. An ad-hoc committee was appointed to look into whether signage was wanted or necessary.

Booth Library is unique in that after entering the building patrons are funneled to the third floor as the main floor of business. The north end of the building is the original building. The center has a wide open atrium with bridges crossing from the historic building into the south portion. The south end has the majority of the book stacks and the main public service desk for circulation. Navigation is tricky until the patrons get to know the building. If a patron moves throughout the library, they must remember to get back to the third floor in order to exit the building. We have many disoriented students at the beginning of the semester!

The public restrooms are not easy to locate due to the tall bookshelves, so patrons seeking the facilities often need to ask where to find them. Some elevators cannot easily be seen as they are in nooks or hidden by bookshelves. We have had people walk right past our public desk on the fourth level and not even realize it is there.

After much discussion by the ad-hoc committee, it was determined that signage is more necessary now than it used to be. Students of this generation are more inclined to text or email, and less inclined to ask a question face-to-face.

BEFORE　　　　　　　　　　　　　　　**AFTER**

We have fewer library employees than we had in 2002, so it is more difficult for our students to find someone to ask for directions. We want to be more inclusive. We want patrons to be more comfortable. We want the signs to be easily noticeable, but not garish. To that end we have been working carefully to provide intuitive, informative signage that respects the integrity of the architectural vision.

We realized that we had no clear signage in our technology and media help area. Now we have a large sign above this space so users can quickly navigate and identify this area.

MILNER LIBRARY, ILLINOIS STATE UNIVERSITY
Paul Unsbee, Director of Library IT Services
Elias Wrightam, User Interface Designer

Milner Library at Illinois State University is a six-floor academic library maintaining over 1.4 million items in its physical collections and offers a wide variety of technology to its patrons. Our previous signage grew organically as needs arose rather than follow an overarching signage strategy. This generated a wide range of signage consisting of varying quality and differing design styles. Over time, the need for a common, standard design approach to signage became apparent as patron confusion persisted.

As a starting point, we focused on technology and equipment/service instructions in forming a common, standard design since it represented the majority of our signage and that signage was overly complex, out-of-date, or nonexistent. We began by touring, taking pictures, and documenting all existing technology signage in the building on a floor-by-floor basis. Using this list, signage was then separated into categories, such as printing, scanning, and instructor station. We then identified common needs which would benefit from a standard approach, the need and purpose of the signage, and the extent to which it needed updating: visual redesign, complete rewrite, or irrelevant and should be removed. Signage was prioritized based on impact on patrons with an emphasis on signage for services with high utilization or frequent patron confusion. The text went through a writing and revision process involving both IT staff and content writers for each category, after which it was handed off to our UX/graphic designer, who created a consistent visual look and feel for the signage.

While we have made great advancements with our signage over the past year, our efforts are ongoing. We have plans to create a full style guide for Milner Library signage—based on lessons learned during the redesign of our technology/equipment signage efforts—which will be used as the basis for all library signage going forward.

CONDUCTING A SIGNAGE AUDIT | 45

Sample signage at Milner Library

DEPAUL UNIVERSITY

Alexis Burson, Humanities and Social Sciences Librarian

The DePaul University Library wanted to improve user experience by updating our signage. There were numerous problems with our existing signs: first, we had no standards or guidelines, i.e., text appeared in a variety of fonts, sizes, and colors; many signs were ripped or faded; some information was outdated or even punitive; and in certain areas, clusters of signs had formed creating "visual noise." The end goal of this project was to ensure the display of a cohesive set of signs that promoted a friendly, welcoming atmosphere, presented accurate information, and avoided overloading patrons with unnecessary text.

As chair of the Marketing and Communications Committee, I launched the project by asking the committee members to read an article in the journal *Weave: Journal of Library User Experience,* titled "Signage by Design: A Design-Thinking Approach to Library User Experience," by Edward Luca and Bhuva

Narayan (volume 1, issue 5, 2016), which we discussed at our initial meeting. We then performed an audit to assess signage throughout the John T. Richardson Library's four floors and our Loop Library. We broke into teams, each taking a section, photographed all signs and added them to a shared document on our library intranet. We categorized each sign, tagged them with "feeling emojis," and separated them into the following categories:

> *Directional:* Helps users orient themselves. Examples: find an area, locate part of collection.
>
> *Informational:* Includes informational and instructional messages. Examples: How to use a machine, perform a task, inform users of things they didn't know about and we want to promote, cart location.
>
> *Regulatory:* Aims to enforce rules and behavior. Examples: No talking, policy signs, etc.
>
> *Fun/Delightful:* Reinforce a positive environment with humor playfulness or creativity.

The committee assigned an action to each category such as update, remove, change to a handout, or redesign then began the design work. The process involved consulting with a number of library departments, gaining buy-in from administration to sanction the project, and convincing committee members that the tedious steps involved in collecting photographs and assessing the collection as a whole was necessary to move forward with a holistic approach.

The outcome was favorable with consistent, current, and friendly signs across two campus libraries. In addition to redesigning all the signs, we created standards and guidelines for future sign development and even created templates for new signs. Most departments have adhered to the guidelines and the committee will continue to provide oversight.

BEFORE

AFTER

UNIVERSITY OF ARKANSAS-FORT SMITH
Jordan Ruud, Public Services Librarian

The first part of our signage audit involved dispensing entirely with some signs we'd had for a long time whose purpose now seemed redundant and unclear. For example, for years we'd had table tents warning students not to leave their belongings unattended. These were barely legible, took up valuable table space, and generally seemed to go unread. We made these disappear.

We were left with a number of signs whose purposes still seemed important—directional signs and signs meant to indicate policy—and our redesigning process proceeded with a few objectives in mind. To start with, we wanted to achieve a sense of visual unity (but without an absolute uniformity that might make signs go unread because they don't stand out). We decided on a base set of fonts for our signs, which depart from software defaults (on the assumption that most signs elsewhere on campus do get printed in fonts like Calibri and therefore don't stand out visually). Next, we consulted our campus's graphic style guide and found a set of preferred colors used for branding. We made these colors the basis of several of our signs in an effort to achieve further visual unity, but we permitted some variation. For example, our sign pointing to "quiet study area" and "group study area" incorporates our campus's signature shades of blue and gold, but also some brighter hues meant to catch the eye further.

Our design process for new signs usually began with our team lead on the signage audit, Edward Portman, designing several drafts, which the staff would then discuss as a group. We took careful stock of wording and graphic elements, and set out to consider specific situations when creating signs. One example was a confrontational sign at the lobby entrance that formerly (and futilely) declared "NO FOOD ALLOWED BEYOND THIS POINT." Our new sign in the same location visually notes which kinds of food we do and don't allow in the library.

BEFORE

AFTER

NORTH HALL LIBRARY, MANSFIELD UNIVERSITY OF PENNSYLVANIA

Sheila Kasperek, Reference Librarian

The North Hall Library at Mansfield University overhauled its signs in 2011 as part of a larger project to improve communication channels. Prior to the redesign process, library signs were created as needed by whomever wanted the sign in whatever style they liked. The aesthetic of the signs varied widely, lacked a uniform look, were often difficult to read, occasionally were photocopies of photocopies, and looked, as a whole, unprofessional. The project to address these issues included all signs created and printed by library employees, which was and is the majority of signs in the building.

Starting with developing a library logo, we then created basic graphic standards specifying a common font and colors for use in library signs. We applied the design principles of contrast, alignment, and repetition as we replaced existing signs with a cleaner, more modern design that was considerably more readable at a distance. With a consistent look to the signs, official library information became easily identifiable. Not only were the signs more professional looking, but their consistency also lent authority to the information.

The largest improvement to the signs came from intentionally identifying the important information on the sign and making that the most visible portion of the sign. Employing contrast effectively, we made sure that the signs' main content could be viewed at a distance, emphasizing the important information. For some signs this meant creating a large bold headline to draw attention so users would know to read the fine print on the sign if needed.

BEFORE

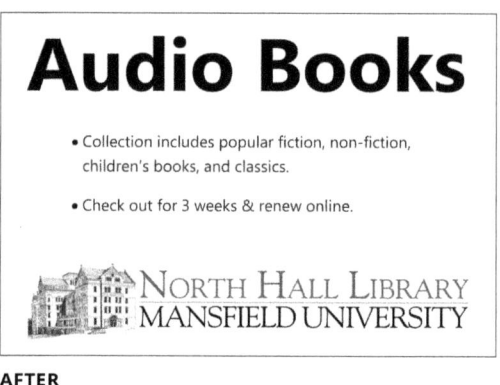

AFTER

CONDUCTING A SIGNAGE AUDIT | 49

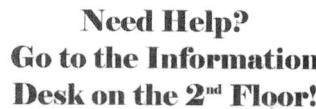

BEFORE   AFTER

For others, it was emphasizing the main meaning of the sign so that users would understand the message quickly with little effort. In many cases, sign size was increased from letter to ledger to accommodate the necessary font size for clarity at a distance.

Approximately eight years after the start of the project, we continue to use the graphic standards and design principles from the original project as we create and update signs. As our comfort with large bold titles grows, we keep increasing contrast to our signs over time, improving our signs with each iteration.

BEFORE   AFTER

UNIVERSITY OF CHICAGO LIBRARY
Kathy Zadrozny, Web Developer and Graphic Design Specialist

The floor maps used by the University of Chicago since 2011 for the Joseph Regenstein Library had a few usability issues, both for the staff and for the patrons. In these older maps, we separated the reading room from the bookstacks, as we originally felt it would aid patrons in finding stacks materials. User testing through the years proved that the separation of a floor into two parts confused our patrons and perhaps hindered their understanding of the distinctions between these areas. Additionally, the entrance for the bookstacks faced in a different direction from the main entrance of the reading room, requiring these two maps of the same floor to have different orientations. This disoriented users and added to wayfinding frustrations for both our online and on-site maps. The old maps also utilized a broad color palette to aid in distinguishing collection types, but no key or visual cues were included to assign meaning. This made the color assignments unknown to our patrons, and in some cases influenced them to assign their own importance.

Prior to implementing updates to our floor maps we created a wayfinding group with the goal to create spatially accurate maps that were ADA compliant and improved wayfinding. Past usability tests were reviewed, and the group determined what further tests were needed versus what previous data was still accurate. The wayfinding group's usability test in 2018 found that combining the reading room with the bookstacks into one floor map did not interfere with how either experienced or inexperienced users found books. During these tests, no other changes were made to the maps besides merging the two sections into one

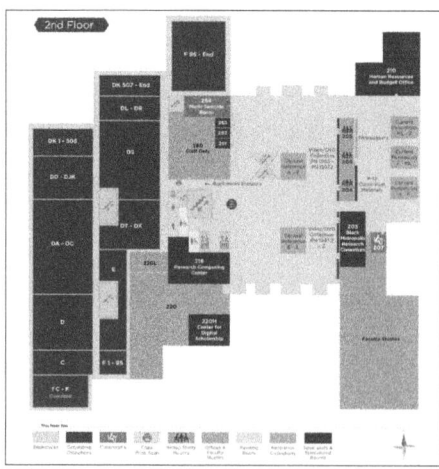
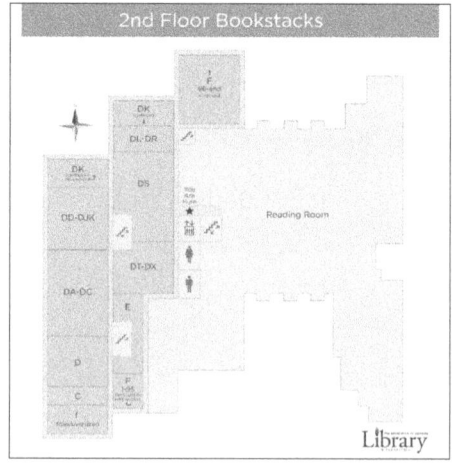

BEFORE **AFTER**

complete floor. However, other data from these testing sessions indicated the need to improve the labeling and visual design.

Motivated by the usability results, we merged the reading room and bookstacks into a single map for each floor, using visual cues to clearly differentiate between the two sections. This allowed us to maintain a consistent cardinal orientation for all maps and reduced the number of online maps from twelve to seven. We then simplified the color scheme to underline locations' commonalities, rather than their differences, which provided a solution to patron confusion about the separate spaces, how they connect together, and what is available in each area. To reduce the color palette, we employed patterns that were tested for color blindness legibility and added a key in a consistent location on all maps.

Lastly, the wayfinding group created guidelines as to what types of items would be shown in a floor map as well as the reasons behind the decision-making process. This documentation helped the group make consistent decisions as to what visual representations were in scope for user-centric floor maps. The updated maps were installed in Fall of 2019 with user tests planned in 2020 to determine if the maps are successful in the wayfinding group's goals.

ROLFING LIBRARY, TRINITY INTERNATIONAL UNIVERSITY
Taylor Wilcox, Electronic Resources Supervisor

In 1974, the Rolfing Library was constructed on Trinity's campus. At the time, the interior design was fresh and modern. Forty-five years later, the style is noticeably outdated and the features of the building do not fully support the demands of today's technology. Even with a limited budget, the library staff have made considerable improvements by shifting materials, opening up more study space, and retrofitting popular areas with additional outlets and lighting. Despite these changes, the entrance to the library was still lacking a warm and welcoming feel.

We desire all of our students to feel at home and comfortable in the library. Many of our graduate students and international students spend significant amounts of time in the library and view it as a community space as well as a study space. We had an idea to paint a mural that would add to the visual aesthetics as well as the community feel. In April of 2019, one of the library staff began brainstorming and sketching concepts for this mural, which would span the 25-foot horizontal space above the circulation desk.

In June of 2019, the mural came to life. Everyone who entered the library was greeted by the phrase "All are welcome" in over 60 languages, each of which is spoken by at least one member of the TIU community. The words form a length of twisted thread, symbolizing the beauty and importance of each language and culture represented. As an added touch, the mural also incorporates ten traditional textile patterns from across the globe. This mural has been highlighted by the campus publications and the local press. It demonstrates to the surrounding community as well as our own students that we are committed to helping them succeed and that we value each and every one of them.

BEFORE

AFTER

NEW YORK LIBRARY OF SOTHEBY'S INSTITUTE OF ART

Lauren M. Puzier, former Acting Head Librarian (now employed at the University at Albany Libraries, State University of New York)

The New York Library of Sotheby's Institute of Art conducted a signage audit and redesign to improve student wayfinding and the browsability of the collection. Sotheby's Institute of Art is a graduate school with academic libraries on campuses in New York and London. In 2016, the New York library, which served about 125 full-time students with a collection of over 10,000 items, underwent a major renovation and redesign. The librarians used this opportunity to evaluate the library signage.

The informational and wayfinding signage on library stacks used a white, US letter-size template and Arial 70-point charcoal font on gray construction paper. Library of Congress call numbers and material types were listed, and a stack number, often used by staff to direct patrons, was placed below the sign on a three-inch by five-inch card. Full-page signs for course reserve books were displayed in acrylic self-standing sign holders placed on shelves. Signs for the library printer included information about other printers on campus and had a busy background and a variety of fonts. The signs used color and graphics inconsistently, and the fonts and style did not align with the institution's brand identity. Some text was difficult to read at a distance. The librarians decided to start afresh after consulting resources on ADA guidance for signage and articles on best practices for creating library signage. They also consulted students and reviewed common questions related to wayfinding that were asked at the service desk. The students indicated a desire for the collection to be more browsable.

To address these issues, a new, flexible sign template was designed that included a graphic element reflecting the contemporary art gallery look and

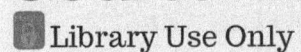

Visual Arts Stack signs

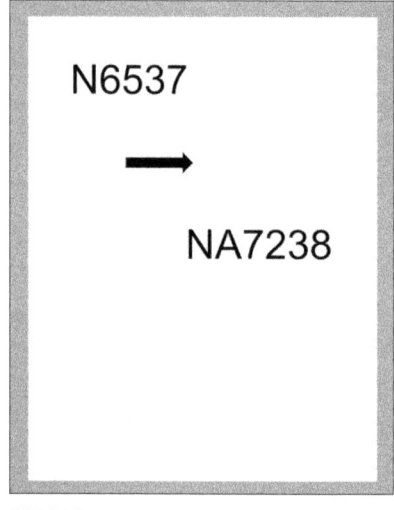

BEFORE AFTER

feel of the building's redesign. The selected serif and sans serif fonts complimented the institution's brand identity, and black text on a white background was chosen for readability. The top of the template highlights important information in large print, with additional information or content below. Examples of additional information include a list of subject headings for each stack range (to increase the browsability of the shelves) and, if applicable, lending rules for specific material types on the shelves. A range number was included on stack signs to help library staff direct students to materials. The template also lends itself to informational signs, such as those near photocopiers and scanners. In the case of signs for the library's printer, the information was pared down to focus only on the printer in the library, with instructions on how to print and make copies. Future versions of this informational sign may be further simplified by editing down the how-to steps and removing subheadings for improved scannability.

UNIVERSITY LIBRARIES AT TEXAS A&M UNIVERSITY
Patrick Zinn, Director of Marketing

Even though signage is such an important part of the user experience for students, faculty, staff, and other visitors to an academic library, our signage had been frozen in time. The signage throughout the buildings was modular but did not utilize common design principles and was expensive to maintain and eventually stopped being maintained. Because of this, the libraries' marketing team saw an opportunity to expand our brand by creating signs relevant and helpful to our users and additionally saw this as an opportunity to brighten old spaces with bright and modern colors. Over time, by being collaborative, knowledgeable, UX focused, and by leveraging our collective expertise, the marketing team was able to become a stakeholder in the development of a new signage program and eventually become the owners of the program across the five libraries.

As owners of the program, the marketing team committed to becoming as knowledgeable about library signage as possible. This included reading articles, visiting other academic libraries, attending library marketing conferences, and speaking with peers. This allowed us to develop an informed view about what a successful signage could and should look like and to understand what signage can and cannot do. Eventually we were able to create signage that met multiple objectives including being informative and UX focused while maintaining accessibility standards both by developing appropriate color contrast and font size.

Starting the program with a UX perspective gave this the freedom to know that the signs would iterate as more knowledge was gained. Because we knew that we would be iterating and looking at what some of the most successful libraries had done, we chose a cost-effective option of vinyl prints to be the medium for our signage program.

As we began to design, we were also able to tap into our student advisory group to get their perspective on our spaces and were able to anchor our design ideas to specific themes that came directly from our own users. For example, in our largest library on campus, the advisory group noted that because all of our

Arrow signage

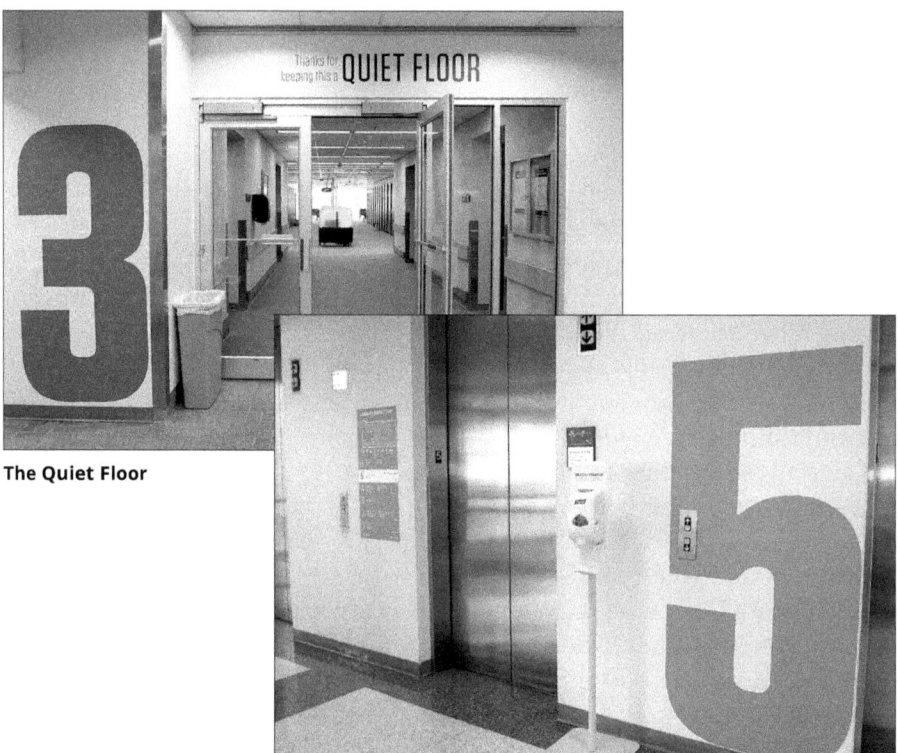

The Quiet Floor

Elevator Signage

landings on our floors looked similar, it was hard to know what floor you were currently on when going up or down multiple floors. As we began to install signage, at various stages, we were also able to use this group for usability tests over time. Their comments allowed us to best understand how users tapped into our signs.

Our signage program has been in place for over two years and our signs include directories on each floor with icons for printers, scanners and computers; arrows above elevators and stairs providing quick information about what is located in each direction; arrows in hallways to direct users to units within the libraries; unit names at their locations; and the locations of significant collections within our spaces.

Our students have provided favorable remarks when assessing the signage, and other visitors have left unsolicited compliments on how helpful the signage has been. Almost as important, the faculty and staff of the libraries have embraced the signage and make a point of sharing stories of seeing student use the signage to find our spaces and services.

BROOKLYN PUBLIC LIBRARY SYSTEM

Karen Sheehan, Executive Vice President, Finance and Administration

Brooklyn Public Library (BPL), the nation's sixth-largest public library system, had last comprehensively updated its interior and exterior signage in the late 1980s and early 1990s. The color scheme was heavily reliant on the system's brand colors of that time (yellow and green), and interior signage was designed to be overly specific to collections and their shelf locations at that time. The design and terminology were outdated, homemade work-around signage had sprung up everywhere, and our branch interiors were not providing the welcoming atmosphere we pride ourselves on providing.

Over the years, budget cuts eliminated funding necessary to keep the signage both accurate and in good condition. As branch hours fluctuated based on funding, and collections shifted and changed, branch staff resorted to creating their own signage. Vinyl lettering detailing branch names and hours became damaged and outdated; one branch had taped twelve years of updated hours of service in layers over their original sign, and metal exterior signage rusted and fell into disrepair. Inside, across the system's portfolio of sixty branches, inconsistent shelving made a single maintenance solution difficult. One particular style, internally referred to as "Waldenbooks shelving" due to their backlit panels, was particularly damaged. Most of the original plastic inserts had cracked or used outdated terminology. Exposed bulbs were visible in nearly half of the shelving, and terms like *Adult Videos* gave the wrong impression. Staff did their best without direction, which resulted in outdated fonts, a mix of terminology and lots of visible packing tape on walls and shelving.

In 2015, BPL's Marketing and Communications team took on the responsibility for updating signage system wide. The goal? To create a cohesive signage system that allowed patrons to easily recognize they were at a BPL branch, find what they needed, and allow staff to keep the signage current and in good condition.

The team took a two-pronged approach. First, we enlisted the assistance of LVCK, an environmental design firm, to design a new exterior signage system that would be as timeless as possible, as well as flexible in anticipation of future operational and branding updates. The kit of parts for exterior signage includes the system name, Brooklyn Public Library, in neutral pin lettering, as well as a signage stanchion with the individual branch's name. This stanchion holds either a static hour of service insert or a digital screen, based on the branch's residential zoning. The screens run on a cloud-based content management system that pulls directly from the branch's web calendar for event listings. Additionally, banner brackets are deployed to make midcentury buildings more noticeable to pedestrians and passing traffic.

Banners currently feature colorful word pairs that help describe what patrons can expect from their library system, and can easily be updated to reflect new programming or branding.

For branch interiors, the marketing team standardized signage holders and terminology. We selected two similar section sign holders for branch perimeters that worked with most shelving, as well as an endcap sign holder that worked on nearly every shelf end.

Additionally, we refreshed all plastic flyer holders across the system to allow staff to promote collections and initiatives without needing to take flyers to walls or shelving.

Working with a team of librarians, we developed a standard set of section signage terms that were descriptive enough to guide patrons but general enough to not need constant updating and shifting. To help further differentiate collections, we distributed shelf clips that branch staff use as needed, with whatever terms they find most appropriate. Additionally, we inventoried all of the interior door signage (restrooms, meeting rooms, facilities, staff areas, etc.). Developing a set of standard room names, we designed new Braille stainless steel signage for all interior doors and used the opportunity to convert single stall restrooms into unisex bathrooms.

Many signage templates are available on BPL's intranet, and staff are able to update their own endcaps and shelf clips; due to the specific size and color, the

BEFORE   **AFTER**

BEFORE   **AFTER**

marketing team provides updated inserts for section signage as needed. While the Waldenbook shelving is slowly being replaced across the system, the marketing team orders new plastic inserts and cuts them down in-house to fit the specific shelf top.

Interior signage guidelines for new or renovated branches simply state that current section signage terms be used for consistency, and that any collections-related signage be easy to update as collections shift and evolve. Some architects have chosen to pull from the guidelines specifically. Exterior signage should be designed using the kit of parts.

BANKIER LIBRARY, BROOKDALE COMMUNITY COLLEGE
Steven Chudnick, Library Director

Due to the unique architectural configuration of the Bankier Library, signage has always been a bit of an issue. With more and more college services such as tutoring and the testing center moving into the library over the past few years coupled with downsizing of staff, we began to notice more and more students getting lost on the way to their destination. With less staff around to monitor the traffic, we decided to produce some more wayfinding guides in house to mixed effect.

You may notice in our *before* pictures the tree and the birds. Although colorful and effective at conveying the intended messages, the material proved flimsy, and some questioned the suitability of such a design in an academic library. In addition, staff always brought up the amount of work needed to swap out signs as closing hours changed in our staff meetings. We had previously asked the College to help us with signage when the tutors first joined us, but all that made it into the budget was the banner sign you can see in the *before* pictures.

Our opportunity to redo the signage came about because of a convergence of several favorable events: the testing center move, the Community College Opportunity Grants (CCOG) offered by the State of New Jersey, a new marketing department, and the availability of Chapter 12 funds. While we were unable to get a proposal readied and signed off on before the CCOG budget year ended, we were able to use Chapter 12 funds to cover the costs. We were happy to work with our new marketing department on this project, and it resulted in a good partnership as you can see in the after pictures. No longer in a rush to finish, we had the time to gather opinions from all stakeholders—staff, administrators, faculty and students—before settling on the final designs. Also, as part of this rebranding, we have aligned our screensavers and other posters by using the new icons. Overall, a great project!

BEFORE

AFTER

BEFORE

AFTER

REFERENCES

Arthur, Paul, and Romedi Passini. 1992. *Wayfinding: People, Signs, and Architecture.* New York: McGraw Hill.

Beck, Susan Gilbert. 1996. "Wayfinding in Libraries." *Library Hi Tech* 14, no. 1: 27–36.

Bosman, Ellen, and Carol Rusinek. 1997. "Creating the User-Friendly Library by Evaluating Patron Perception of Signage." *Reference Services Review* 25, no. 1: 71–82.

Bowler, Leanne, and Andrew Large. 2008. "Design-Based Research for LIS." *Library and Information Science Research* 30, no. 1: 39–46.

Eaton, Gale. 1991. "Wayfinding in the Library: Book Searches and Route Uncertainty." *Reference Quarterly* 30, no. 4: 519–27.

Eaton, Gale, Michael Vocino, and Melanie Taylor. 1993. "Evaluating Signs in a University Library." *Collection Management* 16, no. 3: 81–101.

Etches, Amanda. 2013. "Know Thy Users: User Research Techniques to Build Empathy and Improve Decision-Making." *Reference and User Services Quarterly* 53, no. 1: 13–18.

Gardner, Hollie. 2018. "A User-Centric Approach to Wayfinding Signage." *Public Services Quarterly* 14, no. 4 : 373–85.

Kasperek, Sheila. 2014. "Sign Redesign: Applying Design Principles to Improve Signage in an Academic Library." *Pennsylvania Libraries: Research and Practice* 2, no. 1: 48–63.

Kupersmith, John. 1980. "Informational Graphics and Sign Systems as Library Instruction Media." *Drexel Library Quarterly* 16, no. 1: 54–68.

Johnston, Melissa P., and Lauren H. Mandel. 2014. "Are We Leaving Them Lost in the Woods With No Breadcrumbs to Follow? Assessing Signage Systems in School Libraries." *School Libraries Worldwide* 20, no. 2: 38–53.

Li, Rui, and Alexander Klippel. 2012. "Wayfinding in Libraries: Can Problems Be Predicted?" *Journal of Map and Geography Libraries* 8, no. 1: 21–38.

Luca, Edward, and Bhuva Narayan. 2016. "Signage By Design: A Design-Thinking Approach to Library User Experience." *Weave: Journal of Library User Experience* 1, no. 5. http://dx.doi.org/10.3998/weave.12535642.0001.501.

Mandel, Lauren H. 2009. "Attributing and Defining Meaning to the Built Environment: The Semiotics of Wayfinding." *Proceedings of the American Society for Information Science and Technology* 46, no. 1: 1–6.

———. 2010. "Toward an Understanding of Library Patron Wayfinding: Observing Patrons' Entry Routes in a Public Library." *Library and Information Science Research* 32, no. 2: 116–30.

———. 2013. "Finding Their Way: How Public Library Users Wayfind." *Library and Information Science Research* 35, no. 4: 264–71.

———. 2017. "Wayfinding Research in Library and Information Studies: State of the Field." *Evidence Based Library and Information Practice* 12, no. 2: 133–48.

———. 2018. "Understanding and Describing Users' Wayfinding Behavior in Public Library Facilities." *Journal of Librarianship and Information Science* 50, no. 1: 23–33.

———. 2020. "Comparing Different Methodologies Used in Wayfinding Research in Library Facilities." *Qualitative and Quantitative Methods in Libraries* 9, no. 2: 173–90.

Mandel, Lauren H., and Melissa P. Johnston. 2019. "Evaluating Library Signage: A Systematic Method for Conducting a Library Signage Inventory." *Journal of Librarianship and Information Science* 51, no. 1: 150–61.

Matczak, Jamie. 2018. "Boost! Welcoming, Positive, Consistent Library Signage." *Wisconsin Valley Library Service Newsletter*. www.wvls.org/boost-welcoming-positive-consistent-library-signage/.

Nielsen, Jakob. 2012. "Usability 101: Introduction to Usability." Nielsen Norman Group. www.nngroup.com/articles/usability-101-introduction-to-usability/.

Olin, Jessica, and Joe Hardenbrook. 2015. "Killing It with Kindness, Incorporating Sustainable Assessment through Kindness Audits." Letters to a Young Librarian (blog), March 26, 2015. http://letterstoayounglibrarian.blogspot.com/2015/04/killing-it-with-kindness-incorporating.html.

Passini, Romedi. 1981. "Wayfinding: A Conceptual Framework." *Urban Ecology* 5, no. 1: 17–31.

Polger, Mark Aaron. 2014. "Controlling Our Vocabulary: Language Consistency in a Library Context." *Indexer* 32, no. 1: 32–37.

Polger, Mark Aaron, and Amy F. Stempler. 2014. "Out with the Old, in with the New: Best Practices for Replacing Library Signage." *Public Services Quarterly* 10, no. 2: 67–95.

Roberts, Beth A. 2005. "Library Signage: Creating Effective Signs with Positive Language that Will Get Your Message across to Busy Patrons." *Collaboration for the Dissemination of Geologic Information Among Colleagues* 36: 79–82.

Schmidt, Aaron. 2011. "Signs of Good Design." *Library Journal* 136, no. 2: 17

Schmidt, Aaron, and Amanda Etches. 2014. *Useful, Usable, Desirable*. Chicago: ALA Editions.

Serfass, Melissa. 2012. "The Signs They Are a-Changin'." *AALL Spectrum* 16, no. 6: 5–6.

Symonds, Paul, David H. K. Brown, and Valeria Lo Iacono. 2017. "Wayfinding as an Embodied Sociocultural Experience." *Sociological Research Online* 22, no. 1: 1–20.

Warren, Ruby, and Carla Epp. 2016. "Library Space and Signage Kindness Audits: What Does Your User See?" *Partnership: The Canadian Journal of Library and Information Practice and Research* 11, no. 1: 1–23.

White, Leah L. 2010. "Signage: Better None than Bad." *American Libraries* 41, no. 8 (July): 23.

NOTES

1. See Benedetti 2017; Agosto et al. 2015; Datig 2015; Sonsteby and DeJonghe 2013; Hintz et al. 2010; Ouellette 2011; Castro Gessner, Chandler, and Wilcox 2015; Guo and Goh, 2016; Eichelberger et al. 2017.

2. See, for example, MacDonald 2015; Ellis and Callahan 2019; Pennington et al. 2016; Datig 2015; Rennick 2019; Appleton 2016; Murdoch and Hearne 2014; Walton 2015; Schmidt 2015; Schmidt and Etches 2014.

3. See Gardner 2018; Beck 1996; Eaton 1991; Passini 1981; Li and Klippel 2012; Mandel 2017; Mandel 2018.

4. Some libraries choose digital signage because it is so easy to update, but there are drawbacks to digital signage; see chapter 4.

4
Digital Signage

D IGITAL SIGNAGE (DS) IS A FORM OF ELECTRONIC SIGNAGE, which displays media using illumination (such as fluorescent light, high density display [HID], incandescent light, or neon lighting). Electronic signage is often used to display analog images, beginning when stores would display slideshows of images from analog sources (VHS videotapes playing on VHS players) on cathode ray tube (CRT) television monitors (Bawarsky 2016). DS became more widely available when DVDs and Blu-ray replaced VHS tapes and LCD flat screens became more affordable.

Although framed around advertising, DS can be applied to a variety of environments beyond the retail landscape. Today, digital screens can be found in all sectors of the built environment; airports, train stations, bus terminals, hospitals, college campuses, bars, restaurants, hotels, museums, movie theaters, sports stadiums, subway stations, office buildings—and libraries. According to a 2019 report by market research firm Market and Markets, the digital signage industry was worth $20.82 billion (USD) in 2019 and is anticipated to reach $29.63 billion (USD) by 2024 (Market and Markets 2019).

But what can digital signs offer libraries that print signs cannot, and is that benefit worth the high price of purchase and maintenance? As the next section will show, digital signage has been found in marketing research to have a powerful effect on user mood and perception. In retail settings, the research is clear: there is a statistically significant relationship between certain types of digital signage and positive user experience and emotions. (See Garaus, Wagner, and Manzinger [2016]; Dennis, Newman, Michon, Brakus, and Wright [2010]; Burke [2009]; and Dennis, Brakus, Gupta, and Alamanos [2014]). Many smaller libraries might consider pairing a primarily print signage system with a very limited number of digital signs to display library promotional content or content that changes regularly (such as room numbers for the day's meetings and programming).

Barclay, Bustos, and Smith (2010) show that there are many advantages to using digital signage. Digital signage can be easily updated by multiple staff via a decentralized end-user interface with a web-based content management system. It can display not only text information but graphics and images, including multiple still images that rotate in a slideshow with a preset time interval. It can also display streaming digital media, such as web pages or live feeds of social media platforms such as Twitter. It may also support interactive touchscreen technology, allowing users to directly interact with the system to discover precisely the information they need.

There are multiple types of digital signage, and some may be more appropriate or more useful for libraries than others. According to Schander (2013), there are five decisions to make when setting up digital signage, with the first and most important being whether you will use local or networked signage. There are benefits to each. Digital signage that is standalone (rather than networked) is more cost effective, but it also requires more staff labor to program and maintain. Each digital sign will require a computer monitor and CPU, and each one requires its own software and local storage for digital media. In contrast, networked signage relies on a client-server relationship, with each display monitor playing slides from a centralized media player that is run by a CMS, which may be either in-house or hosted off-site. Networked signage systems are more popular in larger libraries that need to manage a larger collection of digital signs.

If you decide to adopt some digital signage in your library, using best practices can make sure you get the most bang for your buck. Digital signs should always be at eye level, and they work best in high-traffic areas where they can be seen from a distance. Signage content should always be current and timely. Messages should not be text-heavy; the reader should be able to glean the message in three to five seconds. When programming the signs, you should use two different fonts, for contrast (Schmidt and Etches 2014), and you should have a high color contrast between foreground and background (70 percent minimum; Kelly 2011).

If you adopt multiple digital signs in your signage system, the different types of signs should be easily distinguishable; promotional signs should be visually distinct from policy or instructional signs. To distinguish between the different types of signs, assign specific colors to certain types of signs and develop templates that make each sign's purpose. For example, at the College of Staten Island Library, promotional signs were designed in portrait format, while policy signs were designed in landscape (Stempler and Polger 2013; Polger and Stempler 2014).

Components of a Digital Signage System

A successful digital signage system must be a fully integrated, well-planned system, supported by strong, collaborative planning and cohesive content policies and strategies. A digital signage system relies on physical components such as

> *Display monitors* (with or without interactive components): unlike print signage, display monitors with interactive components allow users to engage with the content. (These are separate screens that need to be added to the setup if you decide you want user interaction.) User interaction features may include buttons, touchscreens, facial recognition, and fingerprint recognition.
> *Media players* are small pieces of hardware that use software (a content management system) to display digital signage via one or more display monitor(s) across many locations.
> *Enclosures* are structures that protect the display monitors from damage.
> *Mounting equipment* is used to attach the display monitor to the wall or hang from the ceiling.

Digital signage media players come with their own software, but a suitable content management system must be selected to manage the dissemination of signage content throughout the organization. Customers may prefer to mix and match hardware and software from different companies if they are compatible with each other, but it is often less complicated to select one stable company that offers fully integrated digital signage systems than to search for compatible hardware and software.

Hardware

The categories of hardware associated with digital signage include display monitors, interactive touchscreens, media players, enclosures, and mounting equipment.

DISPLAY MONITORS

Display monitors come in several types. The types most commonly used for digital signage are plasma, LCD, LED, and OLED monitors. Each has its own benefits and drawbacks: plasma monitors are thinnest and have the best picture but are the most expensive; LCD are cheap but they are thick and suffer from burn-in; LED use a lot of electricity; and OLED are expensive to repair.

The following is a selected list of monitors appropriate for typical library display signage uses. There are several types of display monitors you can use for your digital signage.

Cathode Ray Tube (CRT): A CRT uses a beam of electrons to produce an image on a screen (Newton 2014). This type of display is associated with analog-based electronic signage systems and "box-shaped" televisions. Apple stopped producing CRT displays in 2001 and Sony ceased production in 2006 (Newton 2014).

Plasma display panels (PDP): PDPs use ionized gas (plasma) that conducts an electric current; some of the electrical energy is converted into visible light (Liu 2012; Myers 2002). Plasma displays are bulkier and less expensive than liquid crystal display (LCD) or light-emitting diodes (LED) display screens and have higher contrast than LCD screens. Plasma display monitors require higher voltages and currents than other display monitors. They cannot achieve high pixel counts, so they are usually manufactured in large sizes—up to 150 inches diagonally. One of the problems with plasma screens (and CRT displays) is burn-in, which occurs when the same image is displayed on the screen for a long period of time. Since 2010, plasma screens have seen a decline in production, and the LCD and LED market has grown. Both Samsung and LG announced that it will end production of their plasma displays at the end of November 2014 (Bourque 2014; Katzmaier 2014; Whitney 2013).

Liquid crystal display (LCD): LCD monitors use a liquid crystal display with a fluorescent backlight. They are less expensive than LED displays, but they use more energy and are heavier (Wong 2011). The technology is dated, so they are more difficult to find.

Light-emitting diode (LED): LEDs are made of two components: the LCD panel and an LED backlight. The LCD panel contains the pixels, and the LED backlight hits the pixels to display the image. They are more expensive than LCD and plasma displays, but they are lighter and more energy efficient (Kennemer and Waniata 2020; Wong 2011).

Organic light-emitting diodes (OLED): OLED displays produce their own light and color and do not need an extra backlight. They are thinner, lighter weight, and have higher contrasts than LED screens, and are also more expensive. They produce brighter colors and darker blacks (Cohen 2020a). There are two types of OLED displays:

- *Active-matrix organic light-emitting diode (AMOLED)* displays are usually found on smartphones and in larger television displays (from 55 inches to 77 inches). This display uses a thin-film transistor

(TFT) layer that helps the electric current move more quickly along the display, conserving energy (Cabading 2019), and producing a brighter, sharper display.
- *Quantum dot light-emitting diode (QLED)* displays are variations of an LED backlit LCD display; it uses tiny nanoparticles, known as quantum dots, that emit their own light to backlight the display (Cohen 2020b; Katzmaier 2020)

Electroluminescent displays (ELDs): ELDs are flat panel displays that produce high contrast, bright images through electroluminescence: electroluminescent material is laid between two layers of conductors, and the material radiates light when an electric current pass through. Powder phosphor-based electroluminescent panels are used as backlights in LCDs. This is nonthermal light production (unlike incandescent light, where an electric current produces heat that then emits light) (Kretzer 2013).

Electronic billboards (or digital billboards): Electronic billboards are large-scale LED displays that provide dynamic content. These are useful for general advertising or for promoting a time-sensitive campaign; they can also stream live data from websites, TV news, and social media. Electronic billboards are primarily useful for content that must be easily updated, and are likely not cost effective for more permanent, static content. Typically, an electronic billboard will rotate images on an LED screen every six to eight seconds (Hobbs 2018). These large-scale billboards are often designed as POT signs on highways or are used in transit hubs such as airports, train stations, or bus stations or in shopping malls.

Electronic paper (electrophoretic display or EPD): Electronic paper mimics the appearance of ink on paper. It is commonly found in e-book readers, digital wrist watches, microwave oven displays, transit schedules, mobile device display screens, and digital advertising billboards. These displays work best with static images and they can display images without electricity. Electricity is only needed when the content changes. E-paper offers higher resolution, higher contrast, no glare, and greater readability than other displays (Dechaumphai 2007; Primozic 2015a; Primozic 2015b).

Retina displays: Retina displays are a high-resolution LCD display (with an LED backlight) trademarked by Apple and found in various Apple products (iPhones, iPad, Macbook laptops, iMac desktops, and Apple watches). These displays have extremely high resolution (up to 2,436 by

1,125), creating a sharp display where pixels are not visible to the naked eye (Halliday 2020).

The following list includes companies that sell display monitors for digital signage:

3M	Elo	Phillips	Sony
Asus	LG	Samsung	View Sonic
Beetronics	M&T	Sharp	
Cisco	NEC		

Software

Two types of software are needed for digital signage: *the content management system* and *the design software*. The CMS mediates between the media player and the display (both are hardware). It coordinates the dissemination of information to signs, and the *design software* used to create the sign content. Some companies offer "out of the box" signage options that provide entire digital signage systems, including software, local or cloud-based file management, individual or network-based signage solutions, and hosted or local service.

CONTENT MANAGEMENT SYSTEMS

This software organizes the scheduling, flow, and timing of digital signage content (web, images, audio, and video); they pull content from many sources at once and display it instantly on the screen (Harper 2014). Content management systems can be local, meaning all digital files reside on the device, or they can be cloud-based, meaning that the media players connect to the Internet, where all digital sign content is hosted (stored in the cloud). Content management systems are particularly important in large organizations with many signs to be managed. Smaller organizations, like libraries, may use only a few individual, unnetworked signs, bypassing digital signage hosting or expensive content management software and individually managing their digital signs on each display monitor.

Table 4.1 provides a selected list of companies that offer both hardware and content management system software.

DESIGN SOFTWARE

Design software allows you to create the digital content that your signs will display, integrating multimedia such as web-based content (HTML, PHP, ASP pages), video (MP4, WAV, AVI, MOV), audio (MP3), and static images (PNG, JPG, TIFF, GIF) in a seamless way. Familiar examples of design software include

TABLE 4.1

List of companies that provide hardware and content management system software

Hardware and Content Management System Software	Software only
AcquireDigital	Arreya
AdvanTech	BroadSign
AppleTV	Carousel
Arrow: Seneca Media Players	Embed
Box Technologies	Four Winds Interactive
BrightSign	LSquared
Cisco Digital Media Player	Microsoft Digital Signage Software
Demco Proline	
DT Research	Novsign
Elotouch	Omnivex
Engages	Optisigns
Gefen Digital Signage Media Players	Rise Vision
iBase	ScreenCloud
Industry Weapon	Stratosmedia
Kramer Media Players	
Lavacontrols	
LG Media Player	
MediaSignage	
Mvix digital signage players	
NexCom	
NowMicroPlayers	
ONELAN	
OnLogic	
ProLine Digital Signage Players	
Samsung Smart Signage Platform	
Scala	
TouchIT Technologies	
Visionect	
Visix, Inc	
Vivitek USA	
XOGo Mini	
YCD Multimedia Digital Signage Player	

PowerPoint or Adobe Illustrator in addition to the following selected list of design software:

Acquire Digital Editor	Corel Draw	ImTOO MPEG
Adobe Illustrator	Corel Photo-Paint	Encoder
Adobe InDesign	Crello	InkScape
Adobe Photoshop	DesignBold	PicMonkey
Adobe Spark	Desyner	Piktochart
Apple Keynote	FotoJet	Snappa
BeFunky	Fotor	Stencil
Canva	GIMP	

Coherent Strategic Plan and Policy
A fully integrated, seamless digital signage system requires not only hardware and software but also a well-researched, thoughtful strategic plan and strong, coherent policies around signage. A digital signage strategic plan should address sign content, message content and intentions, frequency of message display, and target audience. It should lay out whether signs should be static or dynamic (i.e., live social media posts), who is responsible for creating signs, the specific design (typefaces, sizes, colors) and branding guidelines that must be followed, the number of slides that should be displayed in a slideshow, the time lapse between slides, the scheduling of updated content, and much more.

Types of Digital Signage

There are several library purposes for which digital signage is well suited. Your signage audit should have given you a clear idea not only of what existing signage resources you have but also of what your users need, where your building's pain points are, and what kinds of signage you need to address existing problems. This section provides an overview of the various types of digital signs, classified according to the purposes they serve.

Point of Sale (POS)
Point of sale (POS) signage is used to promote and sell products or services. In libraries, this type of digital signage would be appropriate for library promotions. These types of signs are usually placed at eye level in clear sight lines, such as the end of an aisle of a retail store (Kelsen 2010); in libraries, POS signs should be placed with the services or products that are being promoted. A typical fifteen-second slideshow on a POS sign is comprised of three components: an attractive visual to catch attention (delivered within the first two seconds); a value proposition, such as "free resume workshop!" or "March is Banned Books

month!" (transmitted between seconds three and ten); and a call to action, such as "sign up for the workshop now!" or "check out our banned books display today!" (delivered by the fifteen-second point).

In general, POS signs should be image heavy and low text and should consider *dwell time* (how long users are likely to look at the sign to take in its message). The average dwell time for an individual is 1.5–4.6 seconds, so for a static, noninteractive slideshow, intervals of 5–10 seconds is likely sufficient for users. If POS signs are placed in the recommended locations (at eye level with long sight lines and visible from a distance, such as the end of aisles or long corridors), users' dwell time will increase. Signage in high-traffic areas like exits or entrances will not receive enough dwell time.

Consider user needs and library utilization patterns in scheduling your content. In retail settings, people rarely visit a store on a daily or weekly basis, and POS signs should therefore be updated around once per month to keep content fresh (Kelsen 2010). User research will inform how often patrons visit your library, and whether the same people consistently come at the same times of day. The slideshow (playlist) of digital images that you use in the morning might differ from the slideshow you use in the evening because different users may come during the weekday than in the evening or on weekends. For example, in community libraries, weekday patrons are often retirees and mothers with young children; in the evening and on weekends, patrons often include work-age adults or older children doing schoolwork or meeting with classmates. Tailoring your POS slideshows to reflect the different audiences that visit your library will help meet users' diverse needs.

Point of Transit (POT)
Point of transit (POT) signs are large-scale digital signs intended to grab a person's attention in a short period of time. These types of digital signage include dynamic billboards in Times Square, train and bus stations, highways, and in places where people are in transit. Because users are on the move (and have consequently very short dwell times—less than one second), these signs should be eye catching and contain mostly images and very little text (Kelsen 2010). Ideally, these signs should have no more than five words, rendered in large fonts on a very simple background. In libraries, POT signs might be used for directional information along user pathways; they should be placed near high-traffic areas like entrances and exits, or at decision points like the bottom of the staircase.

Point of Wait (POW)
Point of wait (POW) signs are designed for dwell-time viewers (Kelsen 2010). These are the types of signs that you might expect to find in places where people linger—either in waiting areas (near an elevator or at a service desk) or in

activity areas (like cafes or sitting areas). Creating informative, compelling, entertaining, and interactive content will keep users engaged and interested. These signs can have more text than POT signs because people will have the time to read them. POW signs for waiting areas might be placed near the circulation desk, the reference desk, or the elevator. POW signs for activity areas might be placed in library cafes, silent study areas, the information commons area, or the library computer lab.

Best Practices for Digital Signage

Design Guidelines

CONSIDER VIEWING PATTERNS

When designing signs, consider how users move their eyes across visual content. Using eye tracking devices, researchers found that most users view signs and other digital content in the shape of an "F," scanning (rather than carefully reading) from the top left to the top right, then down the left side, only tracking right when something catches their eye. Eye tracking tests found that when the content is images rather than text, users use a "Z" pattern (Babich 2017a; Babich 2017b). Consider putting the most important information in these visual hot spots.

USE USER-CENTERED VISUAL DESIGN (TYPEFACE, COLOR, COMPOSITION, ETC.)

For the most user-friendly signs, content should be highly visual. A good rule of thumb is the three-by-five rule: either five lines of text with three words per line, or three lines of text with five words per line (Cousins 2015). According to Murshed (2016), signs should have as few words as possible (she suggests fewer than 250 characters—perhaps a bit unrealistic, but try for as few as possible).

Contrast is important in making signs readable and accessible. Color contrast helps text jump out; it refers to the difference between the colors of the foreground with that of the background. Adjacent elements should have at least 70 percent color contrast. Designers should follow the 60-30-10 rule: 60 percent of text should be in one dominant color, 30 percent in a secondary color, and 10 percent in a tertiary color.

Limit each sign to no more than two fonts. Digital signage should use sans serif typeface (such as Arial, Helvetica, and Verdana). Fonts should be large and be able to be seen at a distance: use a 20- to 30-point font for viewers seven feet away and a 100-point font for viewers 26 feet away (Cousins 2015). Use bold rather than italics to emphasize information. Do not use all capitals; they are much more difficult to read (there is not enough contrast between initial capitals and regular text), and all caps can seem aggressive.

Content should be spaced to ensure that the sign does not appear cluttered. Leave enough blank space around the edges for an invisible margin. The text can be either left-aligned or centered; it depends on the type of sign and the amount of text and images on the sign.

Placement and Viewing Distance

There are some basic tenets of placing digital signage: It should be at eye level, it should avoid areas with glare, and it should be in an area with clear sight lines. There are general rules of thumb for placing signs at the proper viewing distance; for example, lobby signs are often placed 10 to 15 feet away from the user, while digital signs in retail settings can be 30 to 50 feet away. But the size of the monitor and the type of media being displayed affect sign placement.

Brown (2015) uses two different formulas to calculate viewing distance. One formula says that the viewing distance should be four times the diagonal height of the digital screen. (For example, a 55-inch display monitor is 48 by 27, or has a 55-inch diagonal height; 4 × 55 = 220 inches, or 18 feet of viewing distance). The other formula calls for a mounting distance of eight times the height of the screen (for example, a 27-inch screen would require a viewing distance of 216 inches, or 18 feet). For text signs, the distance is somewhat closer: the formula for text-heavy signs is a viewing distance of six times the height of the screen (so a 27-inch screen would require a viewing distance of 162 inches, or 13 feet).

Table 4.2 lists the minimum, maximum, and comfortable viewing distances based on screen sizes (NEC Whitepaper, 2019).

TABLE 4.2
Viewing distances based on screen sizes

Minimum distance	Maximum distance	Screen size	Resolution
2 feet	49 feet	50 inches	UHD
2.2 feet	56 feet	55 inches	UHD
2.6 feet	66 feet	65 inches	UHD
2.9 feet	75 feet	75 inches	UHD
3.9 feet	98 feet	98 inches	UHD

The font size should grow with the viewing distance. Always design for at least one inch (72 point) tall fonts for every ten feet of viewing distance; see table 4.3 (James 2017).

TABLE 4.3
Font size based on viewing distances

Letter height	Point Font	Viewing distance (minimum to maximum)
1 inch	72 point	10–50 feet
2 inches	144 point	20–75 feet
3 inches	216 point	30–100 feet
4 inches	288 point	40–150 feet
5 inches	360 point	50–175 feet
6 inches	432 point	60–200 feet
10 inches	720 point	100–450 feet

Assessment of Digital Signage

There are many ways to measure how well your digital signage is reaching your users, from simple, low-cost methods like observation to specialized, expensive measures like eye tracking or facial tracking software. Ducie (2017) recommends observation as one of the most important digital signage metrics, along with the distribution of targeted surveys that assess users' perceptions of your digital signage. Hart (2020) describes an advanced computerized method of tracking engagement: the digital signage company ScreenCloud partnered with Intel's Quividi to create a product that tracked the number of people who passed by digital screens and engaged with the content. (Hart emphasizes that the product use only anonymized facial tracking data—with no facial recognition element—to track the number of people passing by digital screens), their dwell time, and whether they interacted with the digital screen. Bickers (2007) and Ducie (2017) recommend using traffic tracking tools, ceiling cameras, and video recognition software to track how many people stop in front of signage. The following is a selected list of digital signage metric analysis tools:

- 22 Miles
- 3 Divi Analytics
- AVI SPL
- Beabloo Audience Analytics
- Embed Signage
- firmChannel Audience Analytics
- IC touch
- Kanduai
- Media Tile
- Meritec
- Novisign Analytics
- Quividi
- Pixel Inspiration
- SightCorp Digital Analytics Software
- Vaizva

Private-Public Partnerships

Many of these digital signage solutions are expensive, either in employee time and labor or in economic cost. If your library could benefit from expensive software solutions to metric tracking or to networked sign hosting (described in the first section of this chapter), you may wish to investigate partnerships with other organizations to split the start-up costs of digital signage hardware and software. For example, a community library might collaborate with an advertising or signage company on the strategic vision, planning, and implementation of its digital signage; in return for this, the signs might display the name of the advertising company as part of their programming.

One such notable example is the public/private partnership between New York City Transit and private digital signage and computer hardware companies. This partnership produced the popular *On the Go* Travel Stations, located in the Metropolitan Transportation Authority (hereafter MTA) hubs—interactive digital screens built by Intel that provide information to transit riders in New York City (Hurley 2017). These digital kiosks include real-time information for arrival times, coupled with interactive touch screens that contain digital maps and individual route information. These *On the Go* digital signs are the result of a private-public partnership between MTA and two private companies: OUTFRONT (formerly CBS Outdoors) and Intersection (formerly Control Group), both of which specialize in digital outdoor advertising.

Each company designed its own kiosk. OUTFRONT designed an interactive wayfinding kiosk for the everyday commuter by providing an extension to the MTA TripPlanner website. The kiosk provides overall status of the subway service,[1] real-time train departures, and multitouch subway, bus, and rail maps, all of which are ADA compliant. The Intersection kiosk screen is a digital interactive map of the entire subway system, aimed at meeting the needs (identified via market research) of three typical New York City users: locals, commuters, and tourists. Their goal was to provide relevant information efficiently (Lundberg and Zipp 2017). The transit information that each type of kiosk conveys is driven by Mercury, a custom software platform (created by Postlight) that delivers "real time" targeted information in the transit system. Information can be delivered to specific geographic locations based on a specific subway service or line (Metropolitan Transportation Authority 2020). The MTA supplies the data and is responsible for installation and maintenance of the display monitors. There are currently 5,434 screens in the system, with the majority in the subway system. Another 9,000 more screens will be installed in 2022 and by 2023, all 472 subway stations in the city's 5 boroughs will include digital screens. OUTFRONT and Intersection will recoup their investment through advertising revenue (the kiosks show ads for the two companies at periodic intervals).

REFERENCES

Babich, Nick. 2017a. "F-Shaped Pattern for Reading Content." UX Planet, April 4, 2017. https://uxplanet.org/f-shaped-pattern-for-reading-content-80af79cd3394.

———. 2017b. "Z-Shaped Pattern for Reading Web Content." UX Planet, June 16, 2017. https://uxplanet.org/z-shaped-pattern-for-reading-web-content-ce1135f92f1c/.

Barclay, Donald A., Thomas Bustos, and Teal Smith. 2010. "Signs of Success: Digital Signage in the Library." *College and Research Libraries News* 71, no. 6: 299–333.

Bawarsky, David. 2016. "The History and Evolution of Retail Digital Signage." Digital Signage Connection, April 11, 2016. www.digitalsignageconnection.com/the-history-and-evolution-of-retail-digital-signage/.

Bickers, James. 2007. "Tracking Digital Signage Effectiveness." Digital Signage Today, May 9, 2007. www.digitalsignagetoday.com/articles/tracking-digital-signage-effectiveness/.

Bourque, Brad. 2014. "LG Officially Announces Shutdown of Plasma Display Business: Update." Digital Trends, October 29, 2014. www.digitaltrends.com/home-theater/lg-getting-out-plasma-game/.

Brown, Dan. 2015. "How to Choose the Right Digital Signage Size: Content vs. Screen." Rave Pubs, March 12, 2015. www.ravepubs.com/digital-signage-screen-size/.

Burke, Raymond R. 2009. "Behavioral Effects of Digital Signage." *Journal of Advertising Research* 49, no. 2: 180–85.

Cabading, Zach. 2019. "What Is an AMOLED Display?" HP, September 17, 2019. https://store.hp.com/us/en/tech-takes/what-is-amoled-display/.

Cohen, Simon. 2020a. "OLED vs. LED: Which Kind of TV Display Is Better?." Digital Trends, May 11, 2020. www.digitaltrends.com/home-theater/oled-vs-led/.

———. 2020b. "QLED vs. OLED TV: What's the Difference, and Why Does It Matter?" Digital Trends, June 16, 2020. www.digitaltrends.com/home-theater/qled-vs-oled-tv/.

Condomaros, Christina. 2019. "Digital Signage Dwell Time: Secrets that Will Lead You to Success." May 16, 2019. www.yodeck.com/news/digital-signage-dwell-time/.

Cousins, Carrie. 2015. "6 Tips for Designing Signs and Billboards." Design Shack, February 16, 2019. https://designshack.net/articles/graphics/6-tips-for-designing-signs-and-billboards/.

Daviss, Bennett. 1999. "Paper Goes Electric." *New Scientist*, May 15, 1999. www.newscientist.com/article/mg16221864-700-paper-goes-electric/.

Dechaumphai, Ed. 2007. "Electronic Paper: History and Future." Macroelectronics (blog), October 29, 2007. http://macroelectronics.blogspot.com/2007/10/electronic-papers-history-and-future.html.

Dennis, Charles, Andrew Newman, Richard Michon, J. Josko Brakus, and Len Tiu Wright. 2010. "The Mediating Effects of Perception and Emotion: Digital Signage in Mall Atmospherics." *Journal of Retailing and Consumer Services* 17, no. 3: 205–15.

Dennis, Charles, Richard Michon, J. Joško Brakus, Andrew Newman, and Eleftherios Alamanos. 2012. "New Insights into the Impact of Digital Signage as a Retail Atmospheric Tool." *Journal of Consumer Behaviour* 11, no. 6: 454–66.

Dennis, Charles, J. Joško Brakus, Suraksha Gupta, and Eleftherios Alamanos. 2014. "The Effect of Digital Signage on Shoppers' Behavior: The Role of the Evoked Experience." *Journal of Business Research* 67, no. 11: 2250–57.

DeWitt, Debbie. 2019. "How To Maximize Dwell Time For Digital Signage." Sixteen Nine, February 18, 2019. www.sixteen-nine.net/2019/02/18/how-to-maximize-dwell-time-for-digital-signage/.

Ducie, Ryan. 2017. "How to Measure the Impact of Digital Signage." Digital Signage Today, August 1, 2017. www.digitalsignagetoday.com/blogs/how-to-measure-the-impact-of-digital-signage/.

Enis, Matt. 2016. "Signs of the Times." *Library Journal* 141, no. 11: 39–40. www.libraryjournal.com/?detailStory=signs-of-the-times-product-spotlight/.

Garaus, Marion, Udo Wagner, and Sandra Manzinger. 2017. "Happy Grocery Shopper: The Creation of Positive Emotions through Affective Digital Signage Content." *Technological Forecasting and Social Change* 124: 295–305.

Halliday, Fergus. 2020. "What Is a Liquid Retina Display?" PCWorld, August 31, 2020. www.pcworld.idg.com.au/article/646686/what-liquid-retina-display/.

Harper, Luke. 2014. Electronic Signage vs. Digital Signage. Ezine Articles, November 7, 2014. https://ezinearticles.com/expert/Luke_Harper/1765128/.

Hart, Sam. 2020. "We Know If You're Watching: How to Measure Your Digital Signage." ScreenCloud, February 10, 2020. www.insidescreencloud.com/post/how-we-measured-digital-signage/.

Hartman, Forrest. 2020. "LED vs. LCD TVs." Lifewire, February 10, 2020. www.lifewire.com/led-vs-lcd-3276283/.

Hobbs, Lynn. 2018. "Electronic Billboards or Digital Billboards?" Effortless Outdoor Media, May 19, 2018. www.effortlessoutdoormedia.com/electronic-billboards-digital-billboards/.

Hurley, Hanna. 2017. "On the Go Travel Station a Dynamic Public Kiosk Powered by Intel." IoT Integrator, November 8, 2017. www.iotsolutionprovider.com/smart-building/on-the-go-travel-station-a-dynamic-public-kiosk-powered-by-intel/.

Ifhar, Ifti. 2016. "Why Marrying Digital Signage with Location Analytics Is a Winner." ComQi, May 2016. http://comqi.com/wp-content/uploads/2016/05/analytics_whitepaper.pdf.

James, Nelson. 2017. "Signage 101—Letter Height Visibility." Signs blog, July 7, 2017. www.signs.com/blog/signage-101-letter-height-visibility/.

Kasperek, Sheila. 2014. "Sign Redesign: Applying Design Principles to Improve Signage in an Academic Library." *Pennsylvania Libraries: Research and Practice* 2, no. 1: 48–63.

Katzmaier, David. 2014. "Samsung to End Plasma TV Production this Year." CNET, July 2, 2014. www.cnet.com/news/samsung-reportedly-ending-plasma-tv-production/.

———. 2020. "Samsung QLED vs. LG OLED: How the Two Best TV Technologies Compare in 2020." CNET, February 4, 2020. www.cnet.com/news/samsung-qled-vs-lg-oled-how-the-two-best-tv-technologies-compare-in-2020.

Kelly, Liz. 2011. "Applying Clarity to ADA Signage Contrast Requirements." ASI Signage, June 30, 2011. https://asisignage.com/2011/06/30/applying-clarity-to-ada-signage-contrast-requirements/.

Kelsen, Keith. 2015. *Unleashing the Power of Digital Signage: Content Strategies For The 5th Screen*. Amsterdam: Focal Press.

Kennemer, Quentyn, and Ryan Waniata. 2020. "LED vs. LCD TVs Explained: What's the Difference?" Digital Trends, March 31, 2020. www.digitaltrends.com/home-theater/led-vs-lcd-tvs/.

Kretzer, Manuel. 2013. "Electroluminescent Displays." Materiability. http://materiability.com/portfolio/electroluminescent-displays/.

Larson, Kendall, and Allison Quam. 2010. "The Modernization of Signs: A Library Leads the Way to Networked Digital Signage." *Computers in Libraries* 30, no. 3: 36–38.

Liu, David N. 2012. "Plasma Display Panels." In *Handbook of Visual Display Technology*, edited by Janglin Chen, Wayne Cranton, and Mark Fihn, 1139–51. Berlin: Springer. https://doi.org/10.1007/978-3-540-79567-4_74.

Lundberg, Gregory, and Carly Zipp. 2017. "OUTFRONT Media Awarded Long-Term Contract by the New York Metropolitan Transportation Authority for Advertising and Digital Communications Platform across Subways, Commuter Rail and Buses, and Billboards." PR Newswire, September 27, 2017. www.prnewswire.com/news-releases/outfront-media-awarded-long-term-contract-by-the-new-york-metropolitan-transportation-authority-for-advertising-and-digital-communications-platform-across-subways-commuter-rail-and-buses-and-billboards-300526998.html.

Market and Markets. 2019. "Digital Signage Market." Markets and Markets, March 2019. www.marketsandmarkets.com/Market-Reports/digital-signage-market-513.html.

McMorran, Charles, and Veronica Reynolds. 2010. "Sign-a-Palooza." *Computers in Libraries* 30, no. 8: 6–9, 47.

Metropolitan Transportation Authority. 2020. "MTA Deploying 9000 New Digital Screens Systemwide with Real-Time, Location-Specific Information for Customers." July 7, 2020. www.mta.info/press-release/nyc-transit/mta-deploying-9000-new-digital-screens-systemwide-real-time-location/.

Morrison, Geoffrey. 2013. "The Big Picture: Projection Screen Basics." CNET, May 2, 2013. www.cnet.com/how-to/the-big-picture-projection-screen-basics/.

Murshed, Nizia. 2016. "Rules for Digital Signage Copy: Infographic." Mvix blog, April 13, 2016. https://mvixdigitalsignage.com/blog/digital-signage-copy-that-makes-content-engaging/.

Myers, Robert L. 2002. *Display Interfaces Fundamentals and Standards.* Chichester: Wiley.

Naegele, Earl. 2014. "ADA Compliance Considerations in the Digital Signage Industry." PeerSpectives (blog), October 21, 2014. https://blog.peerless-av.com/ada-compliance-considerations-digital-signage-industry/.

———. 2017. "Soaring to Success with ADA-Compliant Airport Technology Solutions." Digital Signage Federation, October 2, 2017. www.digitalsignagefederation.org/soaring-to-success-with-ada-compliant-airport-technology-solutions/#.XynCFRNKhn0/.

NEC White Paper. 2019. "Which Display Size and Resolution Do I Need for a Successful Implementation of Digital Signage Applications?" www.midwich.com/campaign/nec/whitepaper-viewingdistance.pdf.

Newton, David E. 2014. "Cathode Ray Tube." In *The Gale Encyclopedia of Science*, fifth edition, edited by K. Lee Lerner and Brenda Wilmoth Lerner, 825–26. Vol. 2. Farmington Hills, MI: Gale.

Nguyen, Minh T. 2020. "Subway Map." NYC Subway Guide, www.nycsubwayguide.com/subway/subway_map.aspx.

Polger, Mark Aaron, and Amy F. Stempler. 2014. "Out with the Old, in with the New: Best Practices for Replacing Library Signage." *Public Services Quarterly* 10, no. 2: 67–95.

Primozic, Ursa. 2015a. "Electronic Paper Explained: What Is It and How Does It Work?" Visionect, March 15, 2015. www.visionect.com/blog/electronic-paper-explained-what-is-it-and-how-does-it-work/.

———. 2015b. "Nothing Ventured, Nothing Gained: The Versatile History of Electronic Paper." Visionect, March 19, 2015. www.visionect.com/blog/nothing-ventured-nothing-gained-versatile-history-electronic-paper/.

Roggeveen, Anne L., Jens Nordfält, and Dhruv Grewal. 2016. "Do Digital Displays Enhance Sales? Role of Retail Format and Message Content." *Journal of Retailing* 92, no. 1: 122–31.

Schaeffler, Jimmy. 2012. *Digital Signage: Software, Networks, Advertising, and Displays: A Primer for Understanding the Business.* Amsterdam: Focal Press.

Schander, Deborah. 2013. "Digital Signage: A New Tool in Your Arsenal of Knowledge." *AALL Spectrum* 17, no. 5: 7.

Schmidt, Aaron, and Amanda Etches. 2014. *Useful, Usable, Desirable: Applying User Experience Design to Your Library.* Chicago: ALA Editions.

Sellman, Robert. 2020. "Improving Retail Dwell Time with Digital Signage." Omnially, July 8, 2020. www.omnially.com/blog/improving-dwell-time-in-retail-using-digital-signage/.

Silva, Robert. 2020. "Video Projection Screens: What You Need to Know." Lifewire, August 20, 2020. www.lifewire.com/video-projection-screens-1847844/.

Stempler, Amy F., and Mark Aaron Polger. 2013. "Do You See the Signs? Evaluating Language, Branding, and Design in a Library Signage Audit." *Public Services Quarterly* 9, no. 2: 121–35.

Want, Roy, and Bill N. Schilit. 2012. "Interactive Digital Signage." *Computer* 45, no. 5: 21–24.

Whitney, Lance. 2013. "Panasonic to Pull the Plug on Plasma TV Panels." CNET, October 31, 2013. www.cnet.com/news/panasonic-to-pull-the-plug-on-plasma-tv-panels/.

Wong, Philip. 2011. "LED vs. LCD: Which Is Better?" CNET, July 6, 2011. www.cnet.com/news/led-vs-lcd-which-is-better/.

NOTE

1. In New York City, subway "service" and "line" differ. The subway train "service" refers to the specific train route and the "line" refers to the trackage that the train service runs on. Many trains can "serve" on the same track (Nguyen 2020).

5

Signage Best Practices and Policies

THIS CHAPTER OFFERS A SET OF BEST PRACTICES AND GUIDELINES for library signage of all types: directional (wayfinding signage), informational, promotional, and instructional. It also provides examples of different libraries' signage policies to help you arrive at one that works for your specific library.

Libraries are complicated. They have a maze of different departments, a specific method for retrieving books in the stacks, and many different rooms with different purposes: public areas and staff areas, different service desks for different types of materials, and different areas for storing different materials, with varying access policies. Library signs can help guide users through the unfamiliar maze, allowing them to find what they came for with the minimum of anxiety (Eaton, Vocino, and Taylor 1993).

At its most basic, a library signage system should have a directory at the entrance of the building to give users an overview of the layout. Directional signage along high-use channels also aids wayfinding. Identification signage can help users identify different spaces in the library building, telling the user what each space is for so they can discover which space will meet their current information need. Stack signage identifies call number ranges, allowing users to find and retrieve books from the stacks. Other types of signage—promotional, policy, and instructional signage—can help the user discover library services and resources they previously did not know about, understand library policies, and carry out particular tasks (as when an instructional sign is mounted over a copy machine explaining how to use its functions).

Best Practices for Designing Effective Signage

The literature on library signage goes back to an article by Pollett (1976). A simple Library and Information Science Source database search with the search terms *(libraries OR library) AND (signage OR wayfinding)* locates 300 citations to articles from 1976 to the present. Table 5.1 shows the citations breakdown from 1976–2020 from the Library and Information Science Source database.

TABLE 5.1
Citation breakdown from 1976–2020

All	Academic Journal Articles	Magazines	Book Reviews	Book Chapters and Citations to Books	Conference Papers	Unknown Source Material	Dates
41	2	4	9	3	0	23	1976–1986
30	8	5	2	2	0	13	1987–1997
61	24	19	0	2	0	16	1998–2008
168	77	38	6	0	5	42	2009–2020
300	111	66	17	7	5	94	All years

As Table 5.1 illustrates, studies of library signage began in the mid-1970s and rapidly increased after 2008. Studies that discuss design generally agree on two crucial principles about library signage: "less is more" and maintain textual and visual consistency. Articles and books by Pollett (1976), Pollett and Haskell (1979), Kupersmith (1980), Reynolds and Barrett (1981), Mallory and DeVore (1982), Van Allen (1984), Wismer (1988), Eaton (1991), Eaton, Vocino, and Taylor (1993), Johnson (1993), and Boyd (1993) provide the backdrop for this chapter. In the mid to late 1990s, Ragsdale and Kenney (1995), Bosman and Rusinek (1997) wrote about the development of signage systems in libraries, usually researching and reporting student perceptions of libraries, but sometimes discussing the complete overhaul and replacement of signage. Research on library signage has increased in the last twenty years.

Kupersmith (1980) asserts that for library signage to be an effective communication and teaching tool for users, it must be informative, consistent, and user friendly; it should be systematically planned and carried out, following a unified design scheme and reflecting a thoughtful signage policy. Van Allen (1984) cautions against too many signs, particularly ad-hoc signs, as producing visual clutter. While he does not discuss specific design guidelines, he argues that a good signage system is one that properly communicates the institution's intentions, spirit, directions, and its theme. For him, effective signage has four key elements: it should be intelligible, informative, inviting, and inexpensive. Johnson (1993), who describes the process of conducting a library signage replacement project, also notes that fewer signs are more effective, that consistency in signs' wording and design is key, and that signs are most important at key decision points. Other scholarly work sheds light on elements of signage beyond the question of design or user-friendliness. For example, Wismer (1988) offers still-relevant insights into the practical process of soliciting bids from external companies for signage design. The article describes the experience developing a signage system proposal for the Maine State Library system, offering a solid overview of the request-for-proposal process, and a scoresheet for evaluating the bids the library received. The scoresheet measures the proposed signs' overall design, the ease of maintaining this signage system, the ease of installation, the company's experience in developing signage systems, and the completeness of the project bid.

The five best practices of signage design, synthesized from the body of previous work on library signage and on effective signage more broadly, are detailed below.

Make Signs Succinct and Legible

Signs' text should be as brief as possible while maintaining clarity; don't overburden the user with too much information. Redish (2007) recommends using active words and making several passes at editing the text, continuously working to condense your message without losing the meaning. Avoid library jargon; use plain language instead (Polger 2010; Kupersmith 2012). Sign text must be legible both from a reasonable distance and close up. Choose a sans serif typeface.

Finally, avoid handwritten signs. Handwritten signs are often illegible and not ADA compliant, making them inaccessible to some users. While they may be used in emergency situations, they are unprofessional and sloppy, and must be replaced as soon as possible.

Keep User Experience (UX) Design Principles in Mind

Design thinking is a framework that comes from DBR and is often associated with UX design. It seeks to understand the user's needs and preferences through an iterative process that works with the user to identify problems and provide solutions (Dam and Siang 2020; Liedtka 2018; Luca and Narayan 2016). (See chapter 2 for a discussion of some research techniques to discover how users perceive and interact with your library signage.) As Schmidt and Etches (2014) argue in their book on UX and libraries, every library choice should be intentional and have purpose; if you cannot identify the value or purpose of an element of your library (and particularly of a sign), then it should not have been designed to begin with.

Make Text and Visuals Consistent

Because a signage system represents a whole network, or family of signs, you should use consistent language and visual vocabulary throughout, with all signs sharing the same typeface, sizes, and color palette throughout.

Textual and visual consistency may reduce user anxiety and confusion. Prepare a signage policy that includes a design template, style guidelines, and a set of controlled vocabulary (Bosman and Rusinek 1997). The policy should specify which terms to use when *quiet*, *silence*, and *soft conversations* mean different things, and if used synonymously, they can cause misunderstandings (Polger 2014). For familiarity and clarity, use the same consistent design and terms across all promotional and communication channels, such as library brochures, the website, annual report, the newsletter, and social media messages (Polger 2014).

To ensure this consistency, library signage should be planned, evaluated, designed, and implemented by a small committee or working group; the expression "too many cooks spoil the broth" is very true when it comes to library signage.

Design for ADA Compliancy

ADA concerns must be considered in any signage design project. Kasperek (2014), in a thorough account of her library's signage redesign projects, specifically focuses on how to use ADA compliancy standards to create well-designed, accessible signs, discussing color and typeface contrast, color schemata, serif versus sans serif font, alignment, placement, logo design, color, viewing distance, repetition, and composition. (I offer a detailed account of ADA guidelines governing library spaces and signage in chapter 6; here, I give only a very brief set of practical principles for accessible design.)

Kasperek (2014) describes three elements of ADA-compliant design; contrast, alignment, and repetition. ADA compliant signs should have at least 70 percent color contrast. Signage in low lighting areas needs even higher contrasts: adjacent colors must be significantly different from each other in low-light situations (Kasperek 2014). For consistency, include in your signage template the RGB (red, green, blue) or HEX (hexacode) numbers for each of the colors used. Font size contrast is also important: the title section of the sign should have a larger font size than the other sections of the sign (Kasperek 2014).

Alignment is how the text and images are placed on the design canvas. There are psychological differences in how users perceive centered content versus left- or right-aligned content. Titles (or headings) should be aligned to center, and secondary content should be aligned left or right. Alignment also covers bulleting (or chunking) text, which can help with readability.

Repetition is the repeated use of text or image in a particular sign. Repetition can help reinforce the sign's message, but don't go overboard: too much repetition may annoy readers or cause them to tune the sign out.

Placement

For maximum effectiveness, signs must be located strategically, with purpose. Most importantly, signs should be placed where users make decisions; these points should be determined through user research. Polger and Stempler (2014) propose creating a signage locator map, which marks the most appropriate places to mount or display signs to reach the largest audience.

Vary sign design to fit location, which determines how users will engage with the sign. As chapter 4 has detailed, waiting areas such as the line for the circulation desk are suited for POW signs; these signs should contain more text because users will engage with the sign for longer periods of time. For high-traffic areas, POT signs are appropriate; these signs should be highly visual and contain little text because users will probably not stop to read the sign. Promotional or informational signs (POS signs) should be placed in clear sightlines so that library users can see them from a distance.

Signs must be placed at eye height, and the font size should vary with how far the sign is from the viewer. The font size-to-viewing-distance ratio is approximately one inch font height for every 10 to 12 feet of viewing distance. (Text that is one inch high corresponds to 72-point font.)

Other Guidelines to Consider

Number of Signs

Authors unanimously argue that designing fewer signs is better because it helps avoid visual noise (Polger and Stempler 2014; Stempler and Polger 2013; Matczak 2018; Schmidt 2011; Howe and Wilsher 2014, Serfass 2012; White 2010; Luca and Narayan 2016; Bosman and Rusinek 1997; Mandel and Johnston 2014; Mandel and Johnston 2019; Kupersmith 1980; Eichelberger et al. 2017). Sometimes, an overabundance of signs produces inconsistencies; when new signs are simply added on top of existing ones, some of the signage may be outdated, confusing, or contradictory. When library workers create too many signs, they become overwhelming and ineffective. Compounding the problem is the fact that these signs are often negative. The overload of signs expresses library workers' frustration with users who break policies. Sometimes, these workers create signage that scolds users. Similarly, when workers are frustrated with repeated directional questions, they create signs to deflect them—and their frustration comes through. While a lack of signage may result in more reference questions, confusion, and user anxiety, too many signs can result in an environment that is aggressive, unwelcoming, policing, lacks focus, and can cause too much noise.

Revisit Your Signs Often

Remember, signs are living documents that require continuous assessment and revision. Signage systems should not be left to run on autopilot. Keep tabs on your library users' changing needs and ways of using the library. Run periodic research with users; have library workers unobtrusively observe users to assess how they engage with signs; stay aware as your library's pathways and decision points change (Johnson 1993). A monthly sweep of the library's sign locations can be a useful "check-in" to see if signs are clean, in good condition, and in their appropriate places. Reassess signage placement, height, visibility, and sightlines, and check for any new barriers to users seeing or using each sign.

Signs Should Be Professionally Designed

According to a report by the New York State Small Business Development Center (2010), the signage industry is a $4.8 billion market. When you look for a signage company, check whether they are a member of a professional signage association such as the International Sign Association or the US Sign Council. There are full-service signage companies that can survey the physical environment and design, develop, and install your signage. (If you use this type of full-service company, however, you should still conduct user research with your patrons! Most sign companies do not offer this service.)

Signage companies have different specialties: some provide custom built signs, catering to a niche market such as small businesses, while others produce mass quantities of indoor or outdoor signs for larger businesses, like restaurant or hotel chains. If you are unsure which company would be the best fit for your project, there are sign brokers and signage consultants who act as liaisons between you and the signage company. If you choose a signage company that simply manufactures signs to your specifications (not a full-service company), these signage consultants can provide guidance on large-scale signage projects and redesigns.

SIGNAGE MANUFACTURERS

Although this list is far from exhaustive, it provides a small collection of the larger signage companies. To conduct a more comprehensive search, Signsearch (www.signsearch.com) may be used to search and browse local, national, and wholesale signage.

SIGNAGE MANUFACTURERS

- 3M
- Ace Sign Company
- Advance Sign Group
- Atlas
- CAB Signs
- Everbrite
- Fast Signs
- Kieffer
- National Direct Signs
- National Sign
- North American Signs
- Signarama
- Sign Pro
- Signs Now
- Sign Tech
- Signs That Sell
- SmartSign
- Tyson Sign Company
- Vista System
- Walton Signage

SIGNAGE PROFESSIONAL ASSOCIATIONS

- Digital Signage Association
- Digital Signage Federation
- International Sign Association
- Outdoor Advertising Association of America
- United States Sign Council
- World Sign Associates
- World Sign Association

Create a Signage Policy

A signage policy is a document that records the specific parameters of your library's signage, chosen during a signage audit for usability, consistency, and branding. It provides guidelines for style, design, typeface, color schemes (RGB, HTML, or HEX color code), sizing, placement, and the management of the library signage system. It includes a controlled vocabulary, design templates, and image files of your library's logo. It names the stakeholders involved with signage, including the members of the committee or working group that makes decisions about signage. Finally, it lays out processes and schedules for auditing and maintaining all library signage.

The latter part of this chapter contains a sample of signage policies from different libraries, which you can adapt and use as the basis for your own. As you will see, some are very short and succinct, while others are very long and detailed. Some provide extensive samples with typefaces, color schemes, and different variations of their organization's logo. There are samples of signs in both portrait and landscape formats. Many contain guidelines on placement and mounting. Most have clear statements about the mission, goals, and objectives for the signage system. Some provide information on the different audiences they are targeted to. Some contain a statement on the organizational body of individuals who are responsible for the creation and maintenance of these signs. All provide guidelines to ensure ADA compliance.

Sample Signage Policies

The following is a selected list of signage policies from different types of libraries. Some are more succinct, while others are longer and more detailed. Some only focus on digital signage, while others are more general and broader.

EXAMPLE 1: SOUTH CAROLINA STATE LIBRARY SIGNAGE POLICY

Curtis Rogers, EdD, Communications Director

Signage provides information that is not only directional but also promotional, educational, and policy driven. It complements the content on the library website and promotional materials, in addition to the look and feel. A signage policy dictates consistency in language, branding, design, and overall message, thereby promoting user awareness and a visual identity throughout the library. This document defines the types of signs (permanent and temporary), the overall elements of effective design, and sign installation procedures. It provides policies and procedures that relate to the seamless development of effective signage at the South Carolina State Library.

CATEGORIES OF LIBRARY SIGNAGE
- Directional
- Policy
- Informational: educational or promotional
- Labels

DESIGN ELEMENTS
- All categories of signage shall possess a common look and feel. Their message, language, font type, branding, and overall design will be consistent.
- The sign holds a critical message and is considered otherwise unnoticeable to passersby.
- Permission from the Communications Department has been granted.

- *Shape:* General signage will be limited to letter (8.5 × 11) in portrait or landscape, or ledger (11 × 17) in portrait and must be printed on white paper. Permanent signage can be in different sizes and colors, given that consistency is taken into consideration and approval is obtained from the Communications Director or User Experience Designer first.
- *Branding:* Branding will follow the SCSL branding guidelines. The use of the SCSL logo will be employed.

- *Language:* Library jargon and technical language is not permitted. Use plain and simple language, and language must not conflict with library policies. Handwritten signs or labels are not permitted.
- *Message and Tone:* Use positive language where possible. The use of "no" in signage text shall be avoided.
- *Visuals:* Avoid using clipart on signage and be sure to follow copyright laws. Readily common and recognizable icons, logos, or photographs may be used. Please check with the Communications Director or User Experience Designer prior to use.
- *Placement:* Signage should be placed strategically. Signage posted in spaces not approved by a member of the leadership team will be removed. Showing tape on the outside of signage is not permitted. Signage can be mounted using double sided tape or rubber adhesive; however preferred mounting is the use of plastic/acrylic or glass sign frames or holders.

ADA COMPLIANCE

Permanent directional, wayfinding, and room identification signs must be ADA compliant. They should be high contrast and use large fonts. Consult ADA Standards for Braille and tactile lettering, and for the correct positioning of the sign.

REQUESTING LIBRARY SIGNAGE

When creating signage, staff members shall adhere to the signage policy and guidelines. For permanent and special event signs, staff members shall make requests by contacting the Communications Director or the Graphic Designer.

EXAMPLE 2: BROOKLYN PUBLIC LIBRARY BRANDING GUIDE: SIGNAGE

Leila Taylor, Creative Director

EXTERIOR SIGNAGE

Branding the Building: Exterior signage is the face of the brand in the world. With building styles spanning over 100 years, the BPL signage system is an expandable kit of parts that can be adapted to both old and new constructions, creating a coherent and unified brand across the system.

Signage Kit: Components of the signage include the stainless steel-cut out letters for the Brooklyn Public Library building ID, metallic vinyl lettering for the entry ID and address identification, printed fabric banners and standing post signs with the branch name and either digital signage or PVC printed static signage. The components used are dependent on the building type. The color service banner should only be used on older buildings that could benefit from additional graphic presence. They should never be used on Carnegie buildings to maintain the historic integrity of the building. (Carnegie branches use the entry ID and address only.)

Static Branch Signage: Branch signs may be either digital or static depending on the zoning requirements of the neighborhood. The static hours of service sign insert may be replaced as needed.

Digital Branch Signage: Information for digital signs is pulled from the website's calendar of events. Slides include the hours of service, promotional posters, specified programing, and systemwide announcements.

Digital/Alternates Branch Signage: In some instances, vertical signage will be preferred. There is also an option for stainless steel finishes to go with more contemporary architecture.

INTERIOR SIGNAGE

Interior Room Identification
Rooms are labeled in Proxima Nova and Braille.

Section Signs

Used for wall shelving, section signs indicate large general collections such as fiction, nonfiction, early readers, graphic novels, multimedia, or new books. Section signs should be

- 14 × 2.8 (dimensions of sign)
- TYPE Proxima Nova Bold (typeface)
- 82/70 pt (font size)
- All caps (lettering)
- 60 track (tracking)
- COLOR CMYK: 85/70/0/0 (color code)

Shelf clips allow for more specific categorization within a section.

Endcaps are located at the end of shelves and indicate the range of collection. Depending on the size and type of the collection various templates are available for libraries to make their own as needed.

TEMPORARY SIGNAGE: WAYFINDING

Stanchions and A-frames may be provided for temporary wayfinding or to indicate closures.

For temporary announcements or general rules and guidelines, flyers are inexpensive and can be made quickly.

PROMOTIONAL SIGNAGE

Promotional flyers: Flyer templates are available to all staff to promote events, announce closures, or highlight collections. The templates ensure that the correct BPL fonts and logos are used consistently across the system.

Instructional Temporary banners: Large vinyl banners are used to announce branch closings and openings and can be ordered through MACConnect.

Promotional Temporary banners: Large vinyl banners may also be used as exterior signage to promote events or programs.

Temporary signage—promotional flosters: MAC may also do customized flyers or letter-sized (8.5 × 11) posters (flyer posters, or flosters). Flosters may be appropriate for events with several partner organizations, or those likely to have a wider appeal.

EXAMPLE 3: STONYBROOK UNIVERSITY LIBRARIES DIGITAL SIGNAGE POLICY

Janet Clarke, PhD, Associate Dean of Research & User Engagement

The University Libraries' digital signage is used to communicate library-specific information to patrons. Library departments and faculty/staff may request to display information pertaining to library matters such as collections, events, services, news, and staff. All information will be approved for display at the discretion of the Associate Director for Operations and Access Services. The Library reserves the right to edit submissions for digital signage display.

DIGITAL SIGNAGE TIPS
1. Keep it simple and clean! Too much clutter will offend viewers.
2. Best practices for signage applications include clear messaging, limiting the number of characters per slide, avoiding any hyphenated word breaks and using short URLs. A simple background works best with a brief and clear headline.
3. The design elements need to remain within certain safe zones to be viewable on screen. There are two types of safe zones that apply to digital signage: Title Safe and Action Safe.

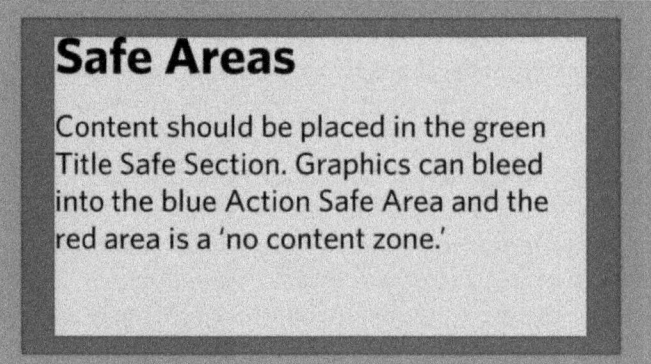

4. Limit the number of words used for copy on each slide. If you need to state a lot of information, consider breaking it up into multiple slides. Twenty to thirty words allow for maximum readability.
5. Recommended type (font) sizes
    - Headlines: 40 points
    - Body copy: 24 points
    - URL/call to action: 28 points
6. Recommended typefaces (fonts)
    - Stay away from serif fonts and/or italics as they don't translate well to the big screen!

Too Much Text

UBC possesses an inspiring openness to ideas, perspectives and ways of exploration that make possible breakthrough thought and discovery. This big-sky thinking has allowed professors and students to carve their own path, try new approaches, and ask the tough questions. One need look no further than remarkable UBC discoveries in the life sciences, leading programs in the Arts, our innovation in technology transfer....

Text Too Small

Audiences are trying to read from distances, busy intersections, and crowded spaces. Make the message bigger so it stands a chance.

Correct Text Size (40 pt)

Recommended text (24 pt)

Headline

Hierarchy has three elements:
1. Headline
2. Body Copy

3. Call to Action

EXAMPLE 4: SYRACUSE UNIVERSITY LIBRARIES DIGITAL SIGNAGE GUIDELINES

Cristina J. Hatem, Director of Strategic Marketing and Communications

SCOPE AND PURPOSE

Digital signage at Syracuse University Libraries is an informational platform aimed at communicating, in real time, what's happening at the libraries and the university. Digital signage keeps the public informed about important events, resources, and services by featuring text, graphics, video, web images, and campus-wide news bulletins on flat-screen HD monitors. In case of emergency, alert messages take precedence over libraries content.

ADMINISTRATION

Content for digital signs is managed by Libraries' Marketing and Communications. Libraries' Information Technology manages the technical infrastructure. Input is periodically sought from Access and Resource Sharing and the Learning Commons. The use of digital signage is subject to the requirements of legal and ethical behavior within the university community.

OBJECTIVES

- To improve engagement and accessibility to libraries'-sponsored and partner events and activities taking place at the library and services/resources offered at the library through visual, easy-to-read screens.
- In the event of an emergency, the university's Department of Public Safety will take over all displays connected to the digital signage.

AUDIENCE

The audiences for the digital signage are all visitors to the libraries, including students, faculty, and staff.

SUBMISSION GUIDELINES

Content will be formatted as a slide within a PowerPoint deck running in the main window of the screen. To submit a request for content to be included in the libraries' digital signage, complete and submit the Digital Signage Content Submission Form.

Content submissions should include:

- Suggested visual image, if appropriate, that is high-quality TIF, PNG, or JPG; at least 1,216 pixels wide by 684 pixels high (and no more than 2,432 × 1,368) in either RGB or grayscale. Please only submit images with copyright approval.

- Recommended headline of three to eight words.
- No more than six bullets/key points.

Marketing Communications reserves the right to edit or decline any suggested content.

EXAMPLE 5: VALDOSTA STATE UNIVERSITY
Laura Bell Wright, Reference and Lending Services Director

SIGNAGE POLICY

Library signage communicates general and specific messages to Valdosta State University students, staff, and faculty. Effective signage empowers library visitors, improves their perception of the building, and assists in navigation.

The members of the Library's Space Utilization and Signage Committee are responsible for identifying needs for new signage and monitoring existing signage. Having clear, uniform signs contributes to the library's mission to support students, staff, and faculty.

Flyers, promotional, and informational materials may be posted by students, groups, and other nonlibrary personnel only on the library's bulletin board located in the Internet Café, near the first floor entrance. These materials must be campus related and approved by the circulation staff before posting. Signage posted without approval will be removed.

Temporary or permanent signs, excluding the bulletin board, must be submitted to the Signage Committee and approved by the Dean of Libraries. Signage posted without authorization will be removed.

EXAMPLE 6: UNIVERSITY OF ILLINOIS LIBRARY DIGITAL SIGNAGE POLICY
Heather Murphy, Chief Communications Officer

University library units/departments and faculty/staff may promote library-related services and events on the library's digital signage at no charge. Signs will appear on a rotating basis throughout the day.

Submit information as a PowerPoint (PPT) slide with a page layout of 18.95 inches wide by 9.58 inches high. Horizontal PDFs or JPGs (300 to 1,080 dpi) are also accepted; please size JPGs to 1,819 by 920 pixels.

- A simple background works best.
- Include a brief, clear headline.
- Twenty to thirty words allow for maximum readability.

- Limit use of small text as it will not be legible on a large screen.
- Only include basic information. Do not go into great detail. Link to a website or other source for details.
- Use of logos or photos pulled from the Internet or other sources may violate copyright law. Submissions may not include any copyrighted images or text without permission.

MANAGEMENT OF CONTENT

The University Library accepts requests to display information on digital signage from Library units and employees pertaining to library matters, including School of Information Sciences (iSchool) events and programs. Departmental libraries may post matters relating to their individual spaces; this could include information about nonlibrary events taking place in a library facility. In addition, any digital signage supporting the library's commitment to diversity and inclusion is acceptable. The library reserves the right to accept/reject requests for digital signs on a case-by-case basis, even in cases where the content does/doesn't match the accepted criteria.

Information is accepted on a first-come, first-served basis. Please allow a week for information to post. Space requests and reservations can be made using the University Library's Digital Signage Request web form below. State the start and end dates information should run through the web form.

Information will be approved for display at the discretion of the Chief Communications Officer.

The University Library reserves the right to edit submissions for digital signage display.

EXAMPLE 7: HESBURGH LIBRARIES, UNIVERSITY OF NOTRE DAME REQUEST AND REVIEW PROCESS FOR DIGITAL SIGNAGE

Cheri Smith, Psychology Librarian and Program Director for the Teaching, Research and User Services Program

First, review the objectives and tiers below and think about how you might want to utilize digital signage.

OBJECTIVES OF CENTRALIZED PROCESS FOR DIGITAL SIGNAGE
- Organize types and functions of signage.
- Standardize and coordinate implementation.
- Brand with official graphics.
- Research trends and implement best practices.
- Help implement signage for stakeholders.

TIERS OF DIGITAL SIGNAGE

Tier One
- Signs designed to help users get directions/wayfind.
- Content is relatively static: information doesn't change often.
- Signs designed for users to get information and go.
- Examples of tier one signs include all number locations, classroom locations, and library or service hours.

Tier Two
- Content is library-driven and features library services, resources, or events.
- Signs are designed to be viewed fairly quickly.
- These signs are changed fairly frequently.
- Examples of tier two signs include signs for library workshops, conferences, exhibits, and highlighted collections.

Tier Three
- Tier three signs feature library-driven content, such as library projects or library collaborations with users.
- These signs feature interactive displays with library content.
- Signs are designed for users to stay, learn, and have an in-depth and interactive experience.
- These signs are infrequently changed.
- Examples include digital exhibits, digital collections, multimedia projects, student work, and student surveys.

CREATE AND SUBMIT A PROPOSAL

Your first step is to create a proposal that answers the following questions:
- What message do you want to convey?
- Who is your target audience?
- Where would you like to display the signage?
- Who is the Facilities Manager for your location?
- Who owns the content calendar?
- Who owns the content creation and management process for your location?
- Do you know if there is funding for hardware and software? Consider:

    Hardware = one time cost (3 year life expectancy on displays)
    Software = $200 year per a screen
    Maintenance
    Internal labor resources
    External Labor Resources

Then, submit the proposal. At the University of Norte Dame, Communications and Marketing review the proposal with Library IT Support Unit (LIBITs), Web and Software Engineering Unit (WSE), and the Digital Signage Team (DST), and then schedule a consultation.

Content creation consultation can begin during the wait period (see below):

- Order Industry Weapon Player.
- Engage Office of Information Technologies to set up a user group, create individual user accounts, and attach them to that group (approximately seven to ten days), etc.
- When hardware arrives, manage installation.

Communications and WSE handle content consultation and creation:

- Work with stakeholders to create templates and custom content.
- Load default content as soon as possible.
- Stakeholders should be trained in signage standards.
- Work with content owners to develop a template system for local content.
- Provide overview of central content and photo assets.
- Local content should be stored in a box folder and loaded into the Industry Weapon database.
- Stakeholders are trained in content management tools, such as Industry Weapon.
- Training review of Adobe Photoshop and Fireworks.

DIGITAL SIGNAGE INTO PRODUCTION
The end user has the ability to update and manage content. Users can:

- Request assistance with new content.
- Request help with Industry Weapon through Service Now (software University of Norte Dame uses to help manage digital workflows).
- Request support for design software through Service Now.
- Request new or custom signage through Communications.

STEWARDSHIP

- Replacement cycles are handled through LIBITs.
- Hardware/software maintenance and management are handled through LIBITs.
- Have a process and owners for spot checks.

EXAMPLE 8: SAINT PAUL'S SCHOOL OF NURSING LEARNING RESOURCE CENTER (LRC) SIGNAGE POLICY

Judy Lee, Learning Resource Center/ Library Manager

Saint Paul's School of Nursing creates promotional, policy, directional, and signs regarding fair use and copyright. Signs are discarded as soon as events have passed, there are policy changes, and equipment is updated. Here are our guidelines for signage:

- Be clear and concise to get the message across easily.
- Get to the point.
- Signage must be timely and should be either updated or discarded if out-of-date.
- Use only the words that are necessary.
- Avoid having signs in all capital letters.
- There should be pretty of white space.
- Avoid clutter. Too much information on the sign makes it confusing.
- Signs should be targeted to staff, students, and instructors.
- The tone should not be demeaning, passive/aggressive, or condescending.
- Make sure that the signs are ADA compliant.
- Signs should be designed vertically and hung at eye level.
- Each sign has a border.
- Use at least size 24 font in a style such as Arial Black, Times New Roman, or Franklin Gothic. Some of our signs use both red and black lettering for emphasis.
- If necessary, use images or graphics to get the message across more easily. From our experience our signs are more easily understood if there are no more than three colors used.
- Images should be copyright free. The source should be listed on the sign.
- Each sign has either the Saint Paul's School of Nursing logo, utilizing our navy and gold school colors or states on the bottom of the sign that it is from "The Learning Resource Center at Saint Paul's School of Nursing."
- If the sign relates to one of the LRC's events, the sponsor, day and time, and activity or activities are indicated.
- Signs for events should be hung on the LRC bulletin board, departmental bulletin boards, and in the student break room (four bulletin boards in this room).

- Our door signs are usually protected by plastic containers and we use painter's blue tape on the signs because scotch tape left behind is difficult to remove.
- Directional signs for equipment should be placed next to the piece of equipment (i.e. photocopy machines and printers).
- We make sure that there are not too many signs displaced up in the same place concurrently.

The selection of sample signage policies represents the different components included in signage policies. The common elements of each policy include design guidelines, placement, messaging, workflow/production, and ADA compliancy. Some are more detailed and specific, while others are more general. There were some libraries who submitted policies that provided many pages of signage templates with style guides that were not included in this chapter because it was too dense and technical. Signage policies can benefit all library workers by providing guidance on the workflow and steps in creating consistent and effective signage that will be placed strategically with a compelling message that adheres to ADA compliancy.

REFERENCES

Berger, Craig. 2014. *Typography, Placemaking and Signs: A Four-Part SFI White Paper Series.* Alexandria, VA: Sign Research Foundation. https://signresearch.org/wp-content/uploads/Typography-Placemaking-and-Signs.pdf.

Bosman, Ellen, and Carol Rusinek.1997. "Creating the User-Friendly Library by Evaluating Patron Perception of Signage." *Reference Services Review* 25, no. 1: 71–82.

Boyd, Debra R. 1993. "Creating Signs for Multicultural Patrons." *The Acquisitions Librarian* 5, no. 9–10: 61–66.

Dam, Rikke Friis, and Teo Yu Siang. 2020. "What Is Design Thinking and Why Is It So Popular?" Interaction Design Foundation, July 30, 2020. www.interaction-design.org/literature/article/what-is-design-thinking-and-why-is-it-so-popular/.

Eaton, Gale. 1991. "Wayfinding in the Library: Book Searches and Route Uncertainty." *RQ* 30, no. 4: 519–27.

Eichelberger, Michelle, Cindy Hagelberger, Stephanie Smith, and Amy Westfall. 2017. "Signage UX: Updating Library Signs for a New Generation." *College and Research Libraries News* 78, no. 10: 560–62.

Howe, Nancy, and Wendy Wilsher. 2014. "Creating Clear and Simple Signage." *Library Journal* 39, no. 15: 19–20.

Johnson, Carolyn. 1993. "Signs of the Times: Signage in the Library." *Wilson Library Bulletin* 68, no. 3: 40–42.

Johnston, Melissa P., and Lauren H. Mandel. 2014. "Are We Leaving Them Lost in the Woods with No Breadcrumbs to Follow? Assessing Signage Systems in School Libraries." *School Libraries Worldwide* 20, no. 2: 38–53.

Kasperek, Sheila. 2014. "Sign Redesign: Applying Design Principles to Improve Signage in an Academic Library." *Pennsylvania Libraries: Research and Practice* 2, no. 1: 48–63.

Kupersmith, John. 1980. "Informational Graphics and Sign Systems as Library Instruction Media." *Drexel Library Quarterly* 16, no. 1: 54–68.

Kupersmith, John. 2012. "Library Terms that People Understand." February 29, 2012. https://escholarship.org/content/qt3qq499w7/qt3qq499w7.pdf?t=m05um6.

Liedtka, Jeanne. 2018. "Why Design Thinking Works." *Harvard Business Review* 96, no. 5: 72–79.

Luca, Edward, and Bhuva Narayan. 2016. "Signage By Design: A Design-Thinking approach to Library User Experience." *Weave: Journal of Library User Experience* 1, no. 5: http://dx.doi.org/10.3998/weave.12535642.0001.501.

Mallory, Mary S., and Ralph E. DeVore. 1982. *A Sign System for Libraries*. Chicago: American Library Association.

Mandel, Lauren H. 2010. "Toward an Understanding of Library Patron Wayfinding: Observing Patrons' Entry Routes in a Public Library." *Library and Information Science Research* 32, no. 2: 116–30.

Mandel, Lauren H., and Melissa P. Johnston. 2019. "Evaluating Library Signage: A Systematic Method for Conducting a Library Signage Inventory." *Journal of Librarianship and Information Science* 51, no. 1: 150–61.

Matczak, Jamie. 2018. "Boost! Welcoming, Positive, Consistent Library Signage." Wisconsin Valley Library Service blog, July 10, 2018. https://wvls.org/boost-welcoming-positive-consistent-library-signage/.

New York State Small Business Development Center. 2010. "What's Your Signage?" https://nysbdc.org/resources/Publications/Whats_Your_Signage_2010_NYSSBDC.pdf.

O'Neill, Kimberly L., and Brooke A. Guilfoyle. 2015. "Sign, Sign, Everywhere a Sign: What Does "Reference" Mean to Academic Library Users?" *The Journal of Academic Librarianship* 41, no. 4: 386–93.

Polger, Mark Aaron. 2011. "Student Preferences to Library Web Site Vocabulary." *Library Philosophy and Practice.* https://digitalcommons.unl.edu/cgi/viewcontent.cgi?article=1650&context=libphilprac.

———. 2014. "Controlling Our Vocabulary: Language Consistency in a Library Context." *The Indexer: The International Journal of Indexing* 32, no. 1: 32–37.

Polger, Mark Aaron, and Amy F. Stempler. 2014. "Out with the Old, In with the New: Best Practices for Replacing Library Signage." *Public Services Quarterly* 10, no. 2: 67–95.

Pollet, Dorothy. 1976. "New Directions in Library Signage: You Can Get There from Here." *Wilson Library Bulletin* 50, no. 6: 456–62.

Pollet, Dorothy, and Peter C. Haskell. 1979. *Sign Systems for Libraries: Solving the Wayfinding Problem.* New York: R. R. Bowker.

Ragsdale, Kate, and Don Kenney. 1995. "Effective Library Signage: A SPEC Kit." SPEC. https://files.eric.ed.gov/fulltext/ED385288.pdf.

Redish, Janice (Ginny). 2007. *Letting Go of the Words: Writing Web Content That Works.* San Francisco: Morgan Kaufmann Publishers.

Reynolds, Linda, and Stephen Barrett. 1981. *Signs and Guiding for Libraries.* London: Clive Bingley.

Rousek, Justin B., and Susan Hallbeck. 2011. "Improving and Analyzing Signage Within A Healthcare Setting." *Applied Ergonomics* 42, no. 6: 771–84.

Sander, John. 2016. "How to Design Effective Display Signs and Billboards." Kool Design Maker (blog), March 14, 2016. http://blog.kooldesignmaker.com/how-to-design-effective-display-signs-and-billboards/.

Schmidt, Aaron. 2011. "Signs of Good Design" *Library Journal* 136, no. 2: 17.

Schmidt, Aaron, and Amanda Etches. 2014. *Useful, Usable, Desirable.* Chicago: ALA Editions.

Serfass, Melissa. 2012. "The Signs They Are a-Changin'." *AALL Spectrum* 16, no. 6: 5–6.

Stempler, Amy F., and Mark Aaron Polger. 2013. "Do You See the Signs? Evaluating Language, Branding, and Design in a Library Signage Audit." *Public Services Quarterly* 9, no. 2: 121–35.

Van Allen, Peter R. 1984. "A Good Library Sign System: Is It Possible?" *Reference Services Review* 12, no. 2: 102–106.

Warren, Ruby, and Carla Epp. 2016. "Library Space and Signage Kindness Audits: What Does Your User See?" *Partnership: The Canadian Journal of Library and Information Practice and Research* 11, no. 1.

White, Leah L. 2010. "Better None Than Bad." *American Libraries* 41, no. 8: 23.

Wismer, Donald. 1988. "Library Signage: Doing It Right." July. https://files.eric.ed.gov/fulltext/ED297755.pdf.

6

Signage and the Americans with Disabilities Act

L IBRARY SIGNAGE, LIKE LIBRARY BUILDINGS, MUST BE ACCESSIble to disabled Americans, including those who are blind, color blind, with vision loss, or who have vision impairment; those with mobility impairments; and Deaf users or users with hearing impairments. Much of this chapter will discuss the legal accessibility requirements for new and renovated public buildings (Arditi 2017). Facility layout and accessibility are intimately related to signage, which (as I have discussed in previous chapters) is crucial to wayfinding. Library signage must help people find their way in the built environment, including to accessible restrooms, elevators, and study areas. This chapter goes into detail on the ADA regulations for accessible signage, which mostly focus on design elements such as typeface, color contrast, character height, width, spacing, and placement, as well as Braille lettering and pictograms.

Brief History of the Americans with Disabilities Act

The Americans with Disabilities Act (ADA) is a civil rights law that prohibits discrimination against individuals with any physical or psychological disability. It was signed into federal law on July 26, 1990, by then-president George H. W. Bush (United States Department of Justice n.d.). It is regulated by the Department of Justice and bans discrimination based on disabilities in programs and services, employment, buildings and facilities, transportation, and communication in the public and private sectors. It provides standards and guidelines for entrances, exits, hallways in buildings, airports, schools, college campuses, shopping malls, buses and subways, as well as guidelines for facility signage (Concannon 2012; Berkowitz 1994). ADA guidelines are continuously updated and revised so the information included in this chapter is based on the 2010 ADA Standards for Accessible Design.

The Americans with Disabilities Act Amendments Act (ADAAA) went into effect on January 1, 2009. The amendments expand the definition of disability to include any impairment that substantially limits one's major life activities (Equal Employment Opportunity Commission 2008).

The ADA grows out of the United States Civil Rights Act of 1964 and the United States Rehabilitation Act of 1973. The first is a civil rights and labor law in the United States that prohibits discrimination based on race, color, religion, sex, or national origin, and specifically prohibits racial segregation in schools, employment, and public accommodations. The legislation was proposed by President John F. Kennedy in June 1963; after Kennedy was assassinated, the bill was pushed through by President Lyndon B. Johnson. The bill was passed and signed into law on July 2, 1964.

Section 504 of the United States Rehabilitation Act of 1973 extends the Civil Rights Act to people with disabilities—one of the first federal civil rights laws to do so. It was designed to protect individuals with disabilities from discrimination based on their disability status. The nondiscrimination requirements of the law apply only to employers and organizations that receive federal financial assistance. This statute was intended to prevent intentional or unintentional discrimination based on a person's disability.

ADA's Five Titles

The ADA is divided into five sections (or titles):

I. The workplace
II. Public services
III. Public accommodations provided by private entities
IV. Telecommunications
V. Miscellaneous

The 1991 ADA Standards for Accessible Design were first published on July 26, 1991, and were revised in the 2010 ADA Standards for Accessible Design (published September 15, 2010). The 2010 standards revised the regulations for Titles II and III, which cover building signage (chapter 2, section 16 and chapter 7, section 703; United States Department of Justice, 2010). On March 15, 2012, these standards became enforceable for all new construction and alterations.

These standards were developed and published by the United States Access Board (also known as the Architectural and Transportation Barriers Compliance

Board), an independent agency of the United States government that developed and maintains the ADA Accessibility Guidelines (ADAAG), which govern the built environment, transit vehicles, telecommunications equipment, medical diagnostic equipment, and information technology. These guidelines form the basis of enforceable accessibility standards used by the Department of Justice (DOJ) and the Department of Transportation (DOT) (United States Department of Justice 2010).

In developing guidelines, the Board follows a multistep process of *rulemaking*, which begins with an advisory committee or regulatory negotiation committee that solicits feedback from stakeholders, then develops consensus recommendations on the substance of a rule and produces a regulatory assessment estimating the rule's costs and other impacts. The rules are approved by the Office of Management and Budget (OMB) before they are published.

Universal Design

The spirit of these standards and rules is expressed in the Universal Design (UD) principles created by the Center for Universal Design at North Carolina State University. According to Mace (2008), UD is defined as design aimed at making products and environments usable by all people, to the greatest extent possible, without the need for adaptation or specialized design. The seven basic UD principles were developed in 1997. The principles are as follows (Apelt, Crawford, and Hogan 2009):

- equitable use
- flexibility in use
- simplicity and intuitiveness
- perceptive feedback
- tolerance for error
- low physical effort
- size and space for approach and use

In lay terms, this means that objects are designed to be usable by as many people as possible; they should allow flexible use to accommodate as many different abilities as possible and to solve as many problems as possible; they should be simple to operate; they should offer physical cues to the user, both about how to use them and about whether they are working; they should allow for user error without penalty; they should require very little physical effort to use; and they should be designed in an appropriate size and placed in such a way that it is accessible.

ADA Guidelines for the Design of Print and Digital Signage

The ADA signage guidelines ensure that persons who are blind or with vision problems can locate and read signs in public and commercial buildings, either visually or through Braille touch (Zelinksi 2018). Current ADA signage laws mandate that signs must accommodate those who read by sight, those who read Braille, and those who read raised characters (Humrickhouse 2012). Users can file a federal lawsuit if they feel that the organization has not met the federal requirements. The DOJ has jurisdiction over local and state governments, and they can award monetary damages up to $55,000 for the first offense and $110,000 for each subsequent offense (Bane 2013).

The ADA has classified four designations of sightedness: normal vision, moderate vision impairment, severe vision impairment, and blindness (Bane 2013). (Moderate and severe impairment are collapsed into the category of *low vision*.) ADA regulates interior signage, requiring accessible signs for floors, stairwells, all exit levels, elevators, restrooms, and all permanent rooms or spaces (Zelinski 2018). It also regulates parking signage, requiring accessible parking spaces to have signs (mounted a minimum of 60 inches off the ground) carrying the international symbol of accessibility. For a parking facility space of seventy-six to one hundred parking spaces, the minimum number of accessible parking spaces is three (standard automobile) and one (van), and at least one of every six accessible parking spaces must accommodate a van. The number of required accessible parking spaces increases with respect to the size of the parking facility (United States Department of Justice 2010.)

ADA Classifications of Signage

The ADA has classified signs into four categories, each of which has specific requirements and guidelines.

The first category is *identification* signs. These signs identify permanent rooms and spaces in public buildings. Examples include restrooms, room and floor numbers, office numbers, and room names. These types of signs must contain tactile or Braille lettering.

The second category is *informational* signs. These are defined as wall-mounted signage that provides information. These are not required to have tactile or Braille lettering, but they must meet other ADA requirements, such as character height, color contrast, and typeface.

The third category is *directional/wayfinding* signage. Like informational signs, directional signs are not required to have tactile or Braille lettering, but they must meet other ADA requirements.

The fourth category is *overhead* signs. These are signs that are projected from a wall or suspended from a ceiling, often identifying exits, elevators, services, and departments. In addition to meeting ADA requirements for height, color contrast, and typeface, these signs must meet height clearance requirements.

ADA Signage Guidelines

Tactile Signage

ADA only requires identification signs to permanent rooms or spaces to be tactile, meaning that these signs must have raised letters, images, or objects on the surface or contain Braille lettering (tactile encoded text that represents natural language). Directional and regulatory signs are not required to contain raised letters or Braille.

However, as Arditi (2017) points out, ADA guidelines are a minimum, not a maximum, and the guidelines do not do enough for users with low, rather than no, vision. Arditi calls for updates to the ADA guidelines, and lays out suggestions for libraries to adopt in the meantime. According to the author, people with low vision (particularly those who lose vision with age) are not trained to read Braille. Signs should be accessible to these visitors, who represent a large proportion of the population: 6.5 million people in 2010, according to the National Eye Institute.

First, Arditi recommends that raised visual signs be in all uppercase letters, which may make it easier for individuals with low vision to read at a distance. Second, he recommends that between the image or pictogram and the sign background on a visual-only sign should have high contrast. Contrast is a percentage calculated from the difference between the minimum and maximum light-reflectance values (LRVs) divided by the maximum LRV. Third, the ADA guidelines do not explicitly mention illumination, so the author recommends that signs be illuminated with both ambient and direct light to increase the legibility of signs and the appearance of contrast.

Pictograms

The ADA requires four types of signs to have pictograms:

- Signs identifying all accessible entrances, restrooms, and bathing facilities if all are not accessible. These signs must display the International Symbol of Accessibility (ISA), the wheelchair.
- Signs identifying the location of the required teletypewriter must display the international symbol of the teletypewriter.
- Signs identifying the location of the required volume control telephone

must display the international symbol for the device, a telephone with lines radiating outward.
- Signs identifying the location of the Assistive Listening System must display the international symbol for that system, an ear with a diagonal arrow behind it.

These four types of signs are required to have tactile lettering (like Braille) below the pictogram. Pictograms should be accompanied with written description below, in the same way that "alt" tags describe the images on websites (Rousek and Hallbeck 2011).

Pictograms are useful for other types of signs, if your budget allows. Pictograms are recommended for restroom signs, and optional for many other types of signs: fire extinguisher, telephone, and drinking fountain signs, handwashing reminder signs, no smoking or no cell phone signs, signs indicating the presence of a baby-changing station or lactation room, and signs identifying the locations of stairs, elevators, and stairwells to be used in case of fire are all optional, but they ensure that low- or no-vision patrons find the library welcoming and accessible.

Ideally, all signs, including pictogram-optional signs, should include tactile lettering such as Braille below the pictogram. When optional pictograms are being used, graphics should follow International Standards Organization (ISO) standards for consistency: the pictograms should be six inches high, text should be three-eighths of an inch high, and raised tactile text should be one thirty-second of an inch high.

Guidelines for Lettering

Sign lettering should be in sans serif fonts, which are visually simpler and less difficult to read at a distance. Signs should not include italics.

ADA guidelines for text character sizes (height and width) are standardized against the height of the typeface's uppercase "I" and the width of its uppercase "O." The vertical span of a letter should be 15 percent of the character height of upper case I—between five-eighths and two inches—and the horizontal span should be 55 to 110 percent of the width of the uppercase O. Letters should have one-eighth of an inch of space between straight sided characters and one-sixteenth of an inch of space between beveled characters (characters with round or sloping sides).

Wall-mounted signs identifying permanent rooms and spaces must include tactile text (Grade II Braille). The height of the tactile text must be between a five-eighths-inch minimum and a two-inch maximum. Its stroke thickness should be a minimum of 10 percent and a maximum of 30 percent of the height of the uppercase I. The character line spacing must be between 10 and 35 percent of the height of the uppercase I. The typeface must be sans serif; characters must not be italic, oblique, script, or any ornate font. The typeface must be nonglare. Contrast between characters and background must be at least 70 percent (Bane 2013).

Ceiling-mounted signs must have font in a matte, nonglare, or eggshell finish that is in high contrast with the background. Braille lettering should be in uppercase letters. The Braille below the sign's text must be three-eighths of an inch from the tactile fonts and three-eighths of an inch from the sign's border (Bane 2013;United States Department of Justice 2010).

Color Contrast
For persons with vision impairment, signage should be designed with high contrast in mind. The ADA recommends a 70 percent contrast between the background and lettering (Humrickhouse 2012). (This seems like common sense, but many designers create signs that are difficult to read, with the background dominating). Building signage should have sufficiently dark text with a white background.

Adjacent colors need to be different from each other so each of the elements of the sign is distinguishable (Kasperek 2014); for signage with colors in the same color family, create contrast within the same color through changes in saturation or brightness.

Signs should also be accessible to colorblind people, who often cannot distinguish blue from yellow, or green from red. Avoiding designing signs with color combinations like green and red, green and brown, blue and purple, green and blue, light green and yellow, blue and gray, green and gray, and green and black. Bright colors are easier for colorblind people to see (DeWitt 2020).

Guidelines for Mounting
Wall-mounted signs identifying permanent rooms and spaces must be mounted on the latch side of the door, with an 18-inch by 18-inch clearance from the door jamb (the vertical portion of the interior door frame). Signs must be mounted straight (with a level) between 48 and 60 inches from the ground, with the center of the sign approximately 54 inches off the ground.

Overhead or ceiling-mounted signs must have an 80-inch clearance from the floor to the bottom of sign.

There are particular regulations governing the installation, display, and content of digital signage systems. Video wall signage screens must be placed between 27 and 80 inches above the floor and must not stick out more than four inches from the wall. The ground space around the screen should be a minimum of 30 by 48 inches. If the screen is too thick, then the wall must be recessed so that the screen can be placed inside (Naegele 2017; Wamaitha 2018).

Interactive digital screens should be mounted between 15 and 48 inches off the ground; they must have touch controls that are mounted no more than 36 to 42 inches off the ground and that are no larger than ten inches of arm's reach in front of the user or to the user's side. Kiosks' interactive touch screens should be installed at a 15- to 20-degree upward slope.

All characters on an interactive touch screen must have at least 70 percent color contrast, be visually different from each other, be nonglare, and be at least three-sixteenths of an inch high; all numeric digits must be in sequence. For users with vision or hearing problems, digital signage must allow users to zoom in to enlarge text, and must have tactile, interactive elements; it must also incorporate voice responsive technology (Wamaitha 2018; Albert 2013; Naegele 2014; Naegele 2017).

Environmental Factors

Spina (2020) identifies accessibility guidelines for library graphic design materials, including environmental factors such as location, lighting conditions, distance from the viewer, and surrounding content. Other design factors include the format (print or online), layout, structure, the use of negative space, and how text and images interact with each other. She also argues that the design should have a hierarchy with different levels of content. Fonts should be readable and avoid all uppercase and cursive, and she recommends using typefaces such as EasyReading, OpenDyslexic, and Dyslsexie. Choosing these fonts may not have an impact of reading speed as there are no conclusive studies that provide evidence (yet) that these fonts are more effective in readability than others. Many like to use color in their graphic design materials, but they should be printing out (or viewing) their finished products in a grayscale version to ensure that the use of color does not impact the overall finished product. Lastly, she states that using nonglare materials and paying attention to contrast is one of the most important design elements that helps increase readability and legibility.

Elevators and Elevator Signage

Elevators are governed by a set of ADA guidelines that address the physical structure, door opening times and durations, button locations, and specific measurements for the distance between the elevator car, door, and floor landing. These ADA guidelines generally apply to elevators in buildings that serve the public, are more than three stories high, and have more than 3,000 feet per floor. However, small medical or professional offices, public transit terminals, or shopping malls are not exempt from ADA guidelines, no matter their size.

There are two types of elevator signage: identification and directional. Identifying signage for the elevator enclosure, the buttons that provide floor designations, and the button controls (door open and close, emergency button) must include both tactile characters and Braille. Elevator buttons should be 42 inches off the ground and three-quarters of an inch in diameter; the tactile characters should be between five-eighths and two inches in height, and Braille must be placed to the left or below the elevator button (Kloepple 2019).

Exit Sign Guidelines

"Means of egress" signs (or exit signs) are directional signs that mark a clear, unblocked pathway to an exit. According to ADA guidelines, egress signage must be all uppercase letters and must have tactile or Braille lettering. They should be in sans serif font and should be at least 48 inches off the ground (Shabluk 2017).

Conclusion: Exemptions from the 2010 ADA Standards for Accessible Design

Exterior signage is exempt from the 2010 ADA Standards for Accessible Design. Other types of signs that are exempt include

- any signage that is in use for less than seven days
- signage in parking facilities (except those identifying accessible parking spaces)
- signage that is used outside of public building space
- seat and row designations in assembly areas
- occupant names
- building addresses
- company names and logos
- building directories
- restaurant menus

Residential Buildings

ADA guidelines only pertain to the public areas in residential apartment buildings. The United States Civil Rights Act of 1964 addressed housing in its Title VIII section (this part is known as the Fair Housing Act, or FHA). When the FHA added amendments in 1988 (known as the Fair Housing Amendments Act of 1988), it addressed some accessibility issues in the design of residential buildings.

The United States Rehabilitation Act of 1973 (section 504) addressed accessibility for newly built rural buildings and the Fair Housing Amendments Act of 1988 provided clarity by identifying seven accessibility requirements for residential buildings. These seven upgrades were required for buildings constructed after March 13, 1988. They are not required to be accessible, but adaptable. They include accessible entrances, public use areas, usable doors, access through covered dwellings, reachable light switches, thermostats, reinforcements for walls, and accessible kitchens and bathrooms. These guidelines pertain to condominium and rental buildings, nursing homes, assisted living facilities, public housing developments, single-family homes with than four or more dwellings, a building with four or more sleeping rooms, carriage house units on an accessible route, townhouses, and units with a loft or raised or sunken living room (United States Department of Housing and Urban Development n.d.; Hill 1999).

REFERENCES

Albert, Rick. 2013. "ADA-Compliant Displays Help Minimize Additional Construction Costs." Rugged Mobility for Business (blog), Panasonic, April 17, 2013. www.ruggedmobilityforbusiness.com/2013/04/digital-signage-displays-ada-compliance/.

Arditi, Aries. 2017. "Rethinking ADA Signage Standards for Low-Vision Accessibility." *Journal of Vision* 17, no. 8: 1–20.

Apelt, Ron, John Crawford, and David J. Hogan. 2009. *Wayfinding Design Guidelines*. Brisbane: Cooperative Research Centre for Construction Innovation.

Bane, Evan. 2013. "A Guide to ADA Signage and Wayfinding Basics." *Doors and Hardware* 77, no. 11: 44–47.

Berkowitz, Edward D. 1994. "A Historical Preface to the Americans with Disabilities Act." *Journal of Policy History* 6, no. 1: 96–119.

Concannon, James. 2012. "Mind Matters: Mental Disability and the History and Future of the Americans with Disabilities Act." *Law and Psychology Review* 36: 89–115.

DeWitt, Derek. 2020. "ADA Guidelines for Digital Signage." Visix, December 1, 2020. www.visix.com/resources/podcasts/dsdr/ada-guidelines-for-digital-signage/.

Equal Employment Opportunity Commission. 2008. "The Americans with Disabilities Act Amendments Act of 2008." www.eeoc.gov/statutes/americans-disabilities-act-amendments-act-2008/.

Introduction to the ADA. n.d. www.ada.gov/ada_intro.htm.

Kasperek, Sheila. 2014. "Sign Redesign: Applying Design Principles to Improve Signage in an Academic Library." *Pennsylvania Libraries: Research and Practice* 2, no. 1: 48–63.

Kinsley, Kirsten M., Dan Schoonover, and Jasmine Spitler. 2016. "GoPro as an Ethnographic Tool: A Wayfinding Study in an Academic Library." *Journal of Access Services* 13, no. 1: 7–23.

Kloepple, Sarah. 2019. "ADA Elevators: What Are the Requirements?." Buildings, November 5, 2019. https://www.buildings.com/articles/34126/ada-elevators-what-are-requirements.

Hill, Michael H. 1999. "The Fair Housing Amendments Act of 1988: The First Decade." *Cityscape: A Journal of Policy Development and Research* 4, no. 3: 57–78.

Humrickhouse, Liz. 2012. "New ADA Signage Standards Take Effect." *American Libraries*, April 25, 2012. https://americanlibrariesmagazine.org/2012/04/25/new-ada-signage-standards-take-effect/.

Mace, Ronald L. 2008. "About UD." The Center for Universal Design, NC State University. https://projects.ncsu.edu/ncsu/design/cud/about_ud/about_ud.htm.

Naegele, Earl. 2017. "Soaring to Success with ADA-Compliant Airport Technology Solutions." Digital Signage Federation, October 2, 2017. www.digitalsignagefederation.org/soaring-to-success-with-ada-compliant-airport-technology-solutions/#.XynCFRNKhn0.

Naegele, Earl. 2014. "ADA Compliance Considerations in the Digital Signage Industry." PeerSpectives, October 21, 2014. https://blog.peerless-av.com/ada-compliance-considerations-digital-signage-industry/.

Rousek, J. B., and M. S. Hallbeck. 2011. "Improving and Analyzing Signage within a Healthcare Setting." *Applied Ergonomics* 42, no. 6: 771–84.

Shabluk, Mike. 2017. "ADA Requirements for Exit Door Signage." Erie Custom Signs, October 26, 2017. https://eriecustomsigns.com/ada-requirements-exit-door-signage/.

Spina, Carli. 2020. "Accessible and Engaging Graphic Design." *Public Services Quarterly* 16, no. 3: 194–99.

United States Department of Housing and Urban Development. n.d. "Fair Housing Act Design Manual." www.huduser.gov/portal/publications/PDF/FAIRHOUSING/fairfull.pdf.

United States Department of Justice. n.d. "Introduction to the ADA." www.ada.gov/ada_intro.htm.

United States Department of Justice. 2010. "2010 ADA Standards for Accessible Design." www.ada.gov/regs2010/2010ADAStandards/2010ADAStandards.pdf.

United States Department of Justice. 2017. "Americans with Disabilities Act Title III Regulations." www.ada.gov/regs2010/titleIII_2010/titleIII_2010_regulations.htm#a304.

Wamaitha, Lilyan. 2018. "How to Make Your Digital Signage ADA Compliant." Mvix blog, November 17, 2018. https://mvixdigitalsignage.com/blog/ada-compliant-digital-signage/.

Zelinski, Alanna. 2018. "ADA Signage All Buildings Must Have." Custom Signs blog, August 28, 2018. www.customsigns.com/blog/2018/08/28/ada-signage-all-buildings-must-have/.

CONCLUSION

Practice What You Preach

YOU NOW HAVE THE TOOLS TO DEVELOP A SIGNAGE PLAN. ONCE YOU HAVE prepared a signage strategy, conducted a signage audit, and crafted a signage policy, you are ready to replace those tired, outdated, and cluttered signs. Your signage replacement project is not just a "facelift" for your library, but it also represents the ever-changing state of your library. Libraries are not stagnant buildings with static services. They are in continuous motion and flux. Services change, collections change, staff change, and policies change. The building ages and needs continuous maintenance. Signs should be seen in that same vein.

When you start your signage audit and replacement, you may choose to consult with a professional signage manufacturer or conduct the whole project in house (my recommendation). Ultimately, your decision is based on your staffing, size of library, budget, and expected project duration. Whatever you decide, it is important to realize that once the old signs have been replaced, they need to be continuously maintained, revisited, and updated. Signs are living documents that inform, communicate meaning, educate, promote, identify, and (attempt) to enforce policy. You cannot do this on your own, so I have provided some advice based on my years conducting signage research and maintaining them in my library.

Practice what you preach. If you are serious about your signage, make sure your library director is on board. To be taken seriously, you need buy-in from them. Having buy-in from your director makes your signage replacement legitimate. In addition, get a team (or committee) together of like-minded colleagues who share your passion. With your library director and small team, you have more leverage to advocate for better signs in your library. This will help your signage efforts so that *most* library workers will collectively and consistently promote the importance of effective library signs.

Be consistent. If you choose to spend time creating compelling promotional signs to promote a service or resource, don't stop with signage. Use the same consistent message on social media, the library website, and on other printed promotions. Signage is just one of many communication tools that are used in conjunction with other tools. For policy signage, make sure that everyone consistently follows the policy and enforces it, or the sign (and policy itself) will be meaningless. For wayfinding signage, promote user-friendly pathways to get from point A to point B. Libraries may be known as mazes and labyrinths, but we need to change our reputation and make our physical facilities easier to navigate. Identification signage should always use plain language and avoid library jargon. If users only engage with our signage for a few seconds, ensure that it is presented using clear, succinct language.

Be friendly. Many of us create signage in response to a policy violation, or because we feel frustrated with our users' behavior. Stop. Library signage should be designed proactively, not reactively. Creating sarcastic, passive aggressive, snarky, and punitive signage may damage your library's reputation and will likely end up on a Google image search for bad library signage. Also, expect your bad signage to appear on a disgruntled library user's social media account. Signage should be welcoming and friendly. Eliminate all caps and make use of *italics* and **bold** instead. Avoid "no" and remain positive. Put yourself in your user's shoes. Get in touch with your feelings. How do you want to feel when you visit your local library? What makes you want to return?

Compromise. Very few of us are solo library workers. I was a solo hospital librarian for several years, so I was my own boss (for many of my daily responsibilities). I worked independently and had to make many decisions on my own. As long as my supervisor (a nurse educator, not a librarian) approved my request, I had free rein. In most professional settings, chances are high that you will be working with colleagues with different perspectives and many points of view. Listen to your colleagues. Agree to disagree and compromise on the best plan of action that will benefit your users, not yourselves. You can cite the library literature until you are blue in the face, but it's important to realize that you cannot win all arguments. Some library staff will want the whole library to be flooded with signs, while others are more apathetic and would be happy to remove them all. There is an argument that library users don't even read signs. The reality is that too many signs may overwhelm your users, while too little signs may result in more questions at the circulation or reference desks. Because each library has its local context and professional work culture, it is best to adjust your expectations and work alongside your colleagues to offer the best solution that everyone can agree on.

Access. Would a person who is blind or who has vision loss be able to access the same information as a person who is sighted? Are you creating equitable means so that all users can benefit from the information you provide in your signs? Think about the size, design, color scheme, and viewing distance of your signs. You might want to protect your signs by having a laminating party, but signs with glare are harder to read.

Do your homework. Conduct ongoing market research and ask your users their preferences to signage messages, designs, and locations. Remember to use different data collection methods. Visit other establishments like airports, train stations, hospitals, restaurants, clothing stores, bookstores, and other libraries. Compare signs and take notes. Are they easy to read and easily understood? Are the wayfinding structures and signs helping you get around, or are you feeling more lost and disoriented?

Be creative and open-minded. Be prepared to make different iterations of your signs. Some text and image combinations will be effective and attract users' attention, while others will not. It's important to be creative, open minded, and patient. Brainstorm different messages and images that will connect with your users. Experiment and watch how your users respond to your library's signage. Your library is its own research lab. Observe your users' behavior, how they wander through the building, and see how they interact with the different touchpoints. These can change over the years. Suspend your prior beliefs and assumptions about your users. You may be surprised to learn that your library and your users evolve, just like the larger world outside.

INDEX

A
A/B testing, xvii, 24
accessibility, 120–121. *See also* ADA compliance
active-matrix organic light-emitting diode (AMOLED) displays, 68–69
ADA Accessibility Guidelines (ADAAG), 109
ADA compliance
    classification of signage and, 110–111
    color contrast and, xvii, 88, 113
    designing for, 88–89
    elevators and, 114–115
    environmental factors, 114
    exemptions from, 115
    exit signs and, 115
    guidelines for, 110
    history of ADA and, 107–109
    lettering, 112–113
    mounting, 113–114
    pictograms, 111–112
    residential buildings and, 115–116
    signage audits and, 17
    signage policy and, 92
    tactile signage, 111
    Universal Design (UD) and, 109
ADA Standards for Accessible Design, 108, 115
advertising, brief history of, 4–5
alignment, 88–89
American Sign Language (ASL), 1
Americans with Disabilities Act (ADA), 107–109
Americans with Disabilities Act Amendments Act (ADAAA), 108
Architectural and Transportation Barriers Compliance Board, 108–109
architectural wayshowing, 6
Arditi, Aries, 111
aspect ratio, xvii
assessment of signage, 35–36
Assistive Listening System, 112
audits. *See* signage audits

B
Bankier Library, Brookdale Community College, 59–60
Barclay, Donald A., 66
Barrett, Stephen, 86
Barthes, Roland, 3
Baudrillard, Jean, 3
best practices
    for designing effective signage, 86–89
    for digital signage, 74–76
    guidelines for, 89–92
    introduction to, 85
bias, types of, 20
Bickers, James, 76
bids, soliciting external, 87
binary questions, 18
biosemiotics, 1
Booth Library, 43–44
Bosman, Ellen, 31–32, 86
Boyd, Debra R., 86
Braille. *See* tactile signage
branding, xvii
Brooklyn Public Library System, 57–59, 94–95
Brown, Carol R., xxi–xxii
Brown, Dan, 75
Brown, David H. K., 7, 34
built environment, xvii
bump points. *See* decision points

124 | INDEX

Bush, George H. W., 107
Bustos, Thomas, 66

C
card sorting, 24
case studies
   description of, 21
   on signage audits, 37-60
   See also individual institutions
categorization/classification of signage, 35-36, 110-111
cathode ray tube (CRT), 68
ceiling cameras, 76
Center for Universal Design at North Carolina State University, 109
Chandler, Daniel, 2, 3
City University of New York (CUNY), 30
Civil Rights Act (1964), 108, 115
classification/categorization of signage, 35-36, 110-111
cognitive mapping, 25
collaborative/cooperative design, 22
College of Staten Island, 30, 66-67
color contrast, xvii, 74, 88, 111, 113, 114
colorblind people, 113
communications, definition of, xvii-xviii
Community College Opportunity Grants (CCOG), 60
compromises, 120
confirmation bias, 20
consistency, 88, 119
content management system (CMS), xviii, 67, 70, 71*t*
contextual inquiries, 18-19
contextual variables, xvi
contrast, xv, 74, 88, 111, 113, 114
copy, definition of, xviii
creativity, 121
cultural probes (reflective documentation), 24

D
decision points, xviii-xix
delome, 2
DePaul University, 45-46
design software, 70-72
design thinking, 30-31, 87-88
design-based research (DBR), 21-22, 87
desirability, 32, 33

DeVore, Ralph E., 86
diary studies (cultural probes), 24
dicent, 2
digital signage
   assessment of, 76-77
   best practices for, 74-76
   components for, 67-72
   description of, xix
   introduction to, 65-67
   references regarding, 78-83
   regulations governing, 113-114
   sample signage policies on, 96-102
   types of, 72-74
directional signage, 35-36, 85, 110, 115
directories, 85
disguised participant observation, 17
display monitors, 67-70
districts, 5-6
dots per inch (DPI), xix
Ducie, Ryan, 76
dwell time, xix, 73
dynamic digital signage, xix
dynamic objects, 2

E
Eaton, Gale, 7, 17, 86
edges, 5
efficiency, 32
electroluminescent displays (ELDs), 69
electronic billboards (or digital billboards), 69
electronic paper (electrophoretic display; EPD), 69
elevators, 114-115
empathy mapping, 23
enclosures, 67
endcap/endcap displays, xix
environmental factors, 114
Epp, Carla, 30
errors, 32-33
Etches, Amanda, 32, 34, 87
ethnographic research methods, 16-19
exemptions, 115
existential facts, 2
exit signs, 115
experience mapping, 23
experiments, 19-20
exterior signage, 115
eye tracking, 20-21, 74

F

Fair Housing Act (FHA), 115
Fair Housing Amendments Act (1988), 115
Farnsworth, Bryn, 21
focus groups, xix, 17
fonts/typefaces
    sans serif, xxii, 4-5, 74, 87, 112, 113
    serif, xxii, 4
    size contrast and, 88
    size of, 112-113
    viewing distance and, 75-76, 89
friendliness, 120
Frutiger, Adrian, 5

G

Goffman, Erving, 7
guerilla testing, 25
Gutenberg, Johannes, 4

H

handwritten signs, 87
Hardenbrook, Joe, 30
hardware, for digital signage, 67-70, 71*t*
Harley, Aurora, xx
Hart, Sam, 76
Haskell, Peter C., 86
Hesburgh Libraries, University of Notre Dame, 100-102
high definition (HD), definition of, xix
Hjelmslev, Louis, 3
Hoch, Devon, 1

I

iconography, 3
icons, 2
identification signage, 85, 110, 111, 115
Illinois State University, 44-45
illumination, 111
Image of the City, The (Lynch), 5
immediate objects, 2
indexes, 2
information design, xvi
information overload, xv, 18
informational signage, 35-36, 110
informational wayshowing, 6
Institutional Review Board (IRB) approval, 15
International Health Facility Guidelines, 8-9
International Sign Association, 90

International Standards Organization (ISO) standards, 112
International Symbol of Accessibility (ISA), 111
interpretants, 2
Intersection, 77
interviewer bias, 20
interviews, 18-19
inventory of signage system, 35

J

Johnson, Carolyn, 86, 87
Johnson, Lyndon B., 108
Johnston, Melissa P., 29-30, 35-36
journey mapping, 23

K

Kasperek, Sheila, 31, 88
Kellaris, James J., xvi
Kennedy, John F., 108
Kenney, Don, 86
kerning, xx
"kindness" signage audits, 30
Kippel, Alexander, 8
Kotler, Philip, xviii, xx
Kupersmith, John, 35, 86

L

landmarks, 5-6
laws, 2
LCD (liquid crystal display) monitors, 67, 68
leading, xx
learnability, 32
LED (light-emitting diode) monitors, 67-68
legibility, 87
lettering, 112-113
Li, Rui, 8
Library and Information Science Source database, 86
Lo Iacono, Valeria, 7, 34
Love Library, San Diego State University, 37-38
Luca, Edward, 30-31, 45-46
Lynch, Kevin, 5-6

M

Mace, Ronald L., 109

Machleit, Karen A., xvi
Maine State Library system, 87
maintenance, 36–37
Mallory, Mary S., 86
Mandel, Lauren H., 6, 15–16, 17, 29–30, 35–36
Manual and Specifications for the Manufacture, Display, and Erection of U.S. Standard Road Markers and Signs, 5
manufacturers, 90–91
maps, 3
Market and Markets, 65
market research, xx
marketing message, xx
Martella, Ronald C., 18, 19
Martin Luther College, 41
Matczak, Jamie, 31
McCarthy, Patrick, 38
measurement bias, 20
media players, 67
mediating processes, xvi
memorability, 32
Mercury, 77
Metropolitan Transportation Authority (MTA), 77
Miedinger, Max, 5
Milner Library, 44–45
moderated usability testing, 25
Mollerup, Per, 6
mounting, 113–114
mounting equipment, 67
movable type printing, 3–4
Muhall, Michael George, xvi
Murshed, Nizia, 74

N
Narayan, Bhuva, 30–31, 45–46
National Eye Institute, 111
naturalistic observation, 16–17
networked digital signage, 66
Neurath, Otto, xvi
New York City Transit, 77
New York Library of Sotheby's Institute of Art, 53–54
New York State Small Business Development Center, 90
Nielsen, Jakob, 32
Nightingale, Florence, xvi
nodes, 5–6. *See also* decision points
nominal questions, 18

North Hall Library, Mansfield University of Pennsylvania, 48–49
number of signs, 89–90

O
objects, 2
observational methods, 16–17
Office of Management and Budget (OMB), 109
OLED (organic light-emitting diode) displays, 67–69
Olin, Jessica, 30
On the Go Travel Stations, 77
Online Public Access Catalog (OPAC), 7
ordinal questions, 18
OUTFRONT, 77
out-of-home advertising, xix
overhead signs, 111

P
participant observation, 17–18
participatory design research (PDR), 22
paths, 5
Peirce, Charles Sanders, 2
personas, xx
Pi Sheng, 4
pictograms, 111–112
Pike, Jennifer, xx–xxi
pixels, definition of, xx–xxi
pixels per inch (PPI), xix, xxi
placement, 75, 89
plasma display panels (PDPs), 68
plasma monitors, 67–68
Playfair, William, xvi
point of sale (POS) signage, 72–73, 89
point of transit (POT) signage, 73, 89
point of wait (POW) signage, 73–74, 89
Polger, Mark Aaron, 30, 89
policies for signage
    creating, 91–92
    description of, xxii
    sample, 92–104
policy signage, xvi, 35–36
Pollett, Dorothy, 86
Portman, Edward, 47
posttest-only control-groups, 19–20
pretest-posttest control-group design, 19–20
printing press, 4
private-public partnerships, 77

professional associations, 90, 91
professional design, 90
promotional signage, xvi

Q
QLED (quantum dot light-emitting diode) displays, 69
qualities, 2
quasi-experiments, 20-26
questionnaires, 18
Quividi, 76

R
Ragsdale, Kate, 86
Redish, Janice (Ginny), 87
referent, 2
Rehabilitation Act (1973), 108, 115
removal and replacement of signs, 36, 87, 119
Renner, Paul, 4
repetition, 88, 89
reporting bias, 20
representamen, 2
research, 121
residential buildings, 115-116
resolution
  common names and parameters of, xxi
  definition of, xxi
  HD versus SD, xix
responder bias, 20
response variables, xvi
retina displays, 69-70
Reynolds, Linda, 86
rheme, 2
Richard III, 4
Rivier University Library, 39-40
Roberts, Beth A., 31
Rolfing Library, Trinity International University, 51-52
rulemaking, process of, 109
Rusen, Ciprian Adrian, xxi
Rusinek, Carol, 31-32, 86

S
Saint Paul's School of Nursing, 103-104
samples of, 92-104
San Diego State University Library, 37-38
sans serif typefaces, xxii, 4-5, 74, 87, 112, 113
satisfaction, 32-33

Saussure, Ferdinand De, 3
Schander, Deborah, 66
Schmidt, Aaron, 31, 32, 87
ScreenCloud, 76
segmentation, xxi
Sejong, King, 4
selection/sampling bias, 20
semiotic triangle, 2
semiotics, 1
semistructured interviews, 18-19
sense, 2
Serfass, Melissa, 31
serif typefaces, xxii, 4
service mapping, 23-24
sightedness, designations of, 110-111
sign vehicle, 2
signage
  best practices and policies for, 85-106
  conceptual framework for, xvi
  digital, xix, 65-83, 96-102, 113-114
  research methods for, 15-28
  sign versus, xxi-xxii
  See also ADA compliance
signage audits
  case studies on, 37-60
  description of, xxii, 17-18
  performing your own, 35-37
  published literature on, 29-32
  user experience (UX) and, 32-34
signage design, xvi
signage locator map, 89
signage policy
  creating, 91-92
  description of, xxii
  sample, 92-104
signification, 3
signifier and signified, 3
signifying elements, 2
signs
  form and content of, 3
  history of, 1-13
  versus signage, xxi-xxii
  theory of, 2-3
Signsearch, 90-91
60-30-10 rule, 74
Smith, Teal, 66
software, for digital signage, 70-72, 71*t*
Solomon four-group design, 19-20
Sotheby's Institute of Art, 53-54
South Carolina State Library, 92-93
Spina, Carli, 114

stack signage, 85
standard definition (SD), definition of, xix
static digital signage, xix
Stempler, Amy F., 30, 89
Stonybrook University, 96-97
strategic plans, 72
structured observation, 17
survey research, 18
Symonds, Paul, 7, 34
Syracuse University, 98-99

T

tactile signage, xxii, 111, 112-113, 115
task completion, 24-25
Taylor, Melanie, 7, 17, 86
terminology, xvii-xxiii
think-aloud method, 24
three-by-five rule, 74
Title VIII, 115
touch points. *See* decision points
tracking, xxii
traffic tracking tools, 76
transcription software, 19
typeface. *See* fonts/typefaces
typography, xxiii

U

undisguised participant observation, 17
United States Access Board, 108-109
Universal Design (UD), 109
University Libraries at Texas A&M University, 54-56
University of Arkansas-Fort Smith, 47
University of Chicago Library, 50-51
University of Illinois, 99-100
University of Manitoba, 30
University of Notre Dame, 100-102
University of Technology Sydney, 40
unmoderated usability testing, 25
US Sign Council, 90

usability, 32-33
usability testing, 25, 50-51
usefulness, 32-33
user experience (UX) design, xxiii, 32-34, 87-88
user experience (UX) mapping, 22-24
user personality traits, xvi
user research, 36
user research software solutions, 26
user-centered design, 33-34, 74-75
utility, 33

V

Valdosta State University, 99
Van Allen, Peter R., 86-87
video recognition software, 76
viewing distance, xxiii, 75, 89
viewing patterns, 74
vision impairment, 110-111
Vocino, Michael, 7, 17, 86
voice responsive technology, 114

W

Warren, Ruby, 30
wayfinding
    ADA compliance and, 110
    definition of, xxiii
    facilitating, 8-9
    history of, 5-9
    library, 7-8
    planning strategy for, 9
    signage for, xvi
    user-centered design for, 33-34
wayshowing, 6
Weave: Journal of Library User Experience, 45-46
White, Leah L., 31
Wilmington Memorial Library, 42
Wismer, Donald, 86, 87
wording, 87

ALATechSource

Learn more and subscribe at
alatechsource.org

Practical and concise, ALA TechSource publications help you

- Stay on top of emerging technologies
- Discover the latest tools proving effective in libraries
- Implement practical and time-saving strategies
- Learn from industry experts on topics such as privacy policies, online instruction, automation systems, digital preservation, artificial intelligence (AI), and more

31901068918871

CPSIA information can be obtained
at www.ICGtesting.com
Printed in the USA
BVHW051334190522
637137BV00002B/4